WHAT A CHAP
REALLY
WANTS IN BED

To Tom

Merry Christmas

Lambourn 2009.

Pete & Brigie

Also published by Merlin Unwin Books
7 Corve Street, Ludlow, Shropshire SY8 1DB, UK
Telephone orders: 01584 877456
Website: www.countrybooksdirect.com

THE TOWNIES' GUIDE TO THE COUNTRYSIDE
Jill Mason £20 Hb
CONFESSIONS OF A SHOOTING FISHING MAN
Laurence Catlow £14.99 Hb

THE BEDSIDE BOOK SERIES:

THE FISHERMAN'S BEDSIDE BOOK
Compiled by 'BB' £18.95 Hb
THE SHOOTING MAN'S BEDSIDE BOOK
Compiled by 'BB' £18.95 Hb
THE RACING MAN'S BEDSIDE BOOK
Compiled by Julian Bedford £18.95 Hb

THE FAR FROM COMPLEAT ANGLER
Tom Fort £16.99 Hb or £14.99 Audio cassette
FISHING UP THE MOON
A personal account of the angling affliction
Harry Parsons £17.99 Hb
PRIVATE THOUGHTS FROM A SMALL SHOOT
Laurence Catlow £17.99 Hb
HOOK LINE & THINKER
Alexander Schwab £17.99 Hb
PRUE'S NEW COUNTRY COOKING
Prue Coats £15.99 Hb (October 2004)
FISHING ON THE FRONT LINE
Nick Sawyer £17.99 (October 2004)

Giles Catchpole & Roderick Emery

WHAT A CHAP REALLY WANTS IN BED

A SHOOTING & FISHING BOOK

Illustrated by Olly Copplestone

Merlin Unwin Books

First published in Great Britain by Merlin Unwin Books, 2004

Reprinted 2005

MERLIN UNWIN BOOKS
7 Corve Street, Ludlow
Shropshire SY8 1DB, U.K.
Tel 01584 877456
Fax 01584 877457
email: books@merlinunwin.co.uk
website: www.merlinunwin.co.uk

British Library Cataloguing in Publication Data:
A catalogue record for this book is available from
the British Library

ISBN 1-873674-805

Designed and typeset by R Squared Design, Shropshire.
Printed in the United Kingdom at the University Press,
Cambridge

Contents

Acknowledgements

Boundless thanks are due to Sandy Leventon, Editor of *Trout and Salmon*, for permitting Giles Catchpole's fishing pieces to be included in this anthology and for encouraging them to be written in the first place.

Mike Barnes, the former publisher, and for many years Editor, of *The Shooting Gazette* met Roderick Emery, for the first and only time, while shooting at Grimsthorpe Castle in Lincolnshire and sincere thanks are due to him for permission to reproduce the shooting pieces from *The Shooting Gazette*.

Foreword

by Liz Kershaw, former Publishing Director of *Cosmopolitan* magazine

When I was the publisher of *Cosmopolitan* in the 1990s a good deal of our time and many of our pages were devoted to the question of what men really wanted in bed. I'm not sure that we ever found an answer; indeed I'm not wholly sure that there is one. At least not a solution that will, in the great scheme of things, be "all things to all men".

However there is now at least a partial answer that may be applied to an important sub-set of the species – to wit, Chaps. And what a Chap really wants in bed is, as the subtitle of this book succinctly puts it, a book of shooting and fishing stories.

Given that shooting and fishing are what Chaps do and what Chaps talk about most of the time, and the method by which Chaps measure other people to boot, their need for this book should not come as a surprise. It is a very funny book whose wry humour and witty illustrations provoke consistent chuckling and occasional gut-wrenching guffaws that will make a Chap nose-job the claret.

What is perhaps more important, not least to those who have tried and failed to arouse the interest of a Chap in other arenas, is the insight these pieces give to the rest of us into the inner workings of a Chap's mind.

It is not only, apparently, simply about the pursuit of fish or fowl, less still about rods and guns and tools and technique, it has to do with the mind-set of a certain sort of Chap - the sort of Chap which the authors, and their chums, manifestly are - and who would not recognise a mind-set if it leapt out of a bush and bit them.

But not all men are Chaps and all Chaps are not necessarily men which means that some who will be whiling away many happy hours in bed with this book, instead of any number of the things we tried and tested at *Cosmopolitan*, will be women – which makes the whole issue more complicated than ever.

If I were you, and I probably was, more or less, before I discovered the pleasures of shooting and fishing, I would simply stop worrying about the whole thing and settle down with a damned good book. Like this one.

Liz Kershaw
National Magazine House, May 2004

For all those who invite us,
put us up,
and put up with us.

GC & RE

Beyond Cure

I was asked, the other day, as you are from time to time: Why do you do it? The fact that we were standing in a particularly claggy Fenland field, in the teeth of some particularly vicious Fenland sleet in the rather vague and improbable hope of encircling some of those especially canny Fenland pheasants who had been dotting the landscape some minutes ago but which seemed now to be somewhere else, and that the question was being posed by a very fetching, if somewhat soggy, sceptical girl of recent acquaintance in whose none too distant future I had some ambitions to loom large and longing, gave me cause for a proper consideration of the answer.

Why do people sleep on the pavement outside department stores, in ghastly conditions, for days and nights before the January sales? Just in order to get 15% off the latest fridge-freezer. Why do devoted fans queue for days in order to get a ticket for this concert or that show, when for a

We are all bonkers.

11

fraction of the price they could secure an adequate CD for listening to in the comfort of their own homes? Why pay well over the odds to be at the match you could better watch on the sofa? Why pay serious amounts of dosh to stand in a field in freezing rain? Why stand in a bobble hat on the end of Platform 19 at Crewe with a notebook and an Instamatic?

The answer, of course, is that we are all to some extent or other as mad as snakes and if we did not channel our personal and particular madnesses into what we laughably call a hobby, then the rest of the world would quickly recognise the fact that we are, none of us, more than a fine line away from picking spots of light off the wallpaper and putting them in a basket and would waste no time flat in heaving us into a padded cell and throwing away the key.

The interesting part though, given that we are all - without exception - inclined to undertake something which others see as odd, is who would be strapped into the stiff white overcoats first. You may take the view that the painstaking accumulation of the 15 different versions of Manchester United's away strip - in their original plastic bags, mark you - at several bundles of notes a pop, stored in a cupboard at a controlled humidity and never otherwise used, beyond a very occasional secret fondle on high days and holidays - that this is a pretty bizarre way to carry on. And I would not be slow to agree with you. You might also arch the eyebrow if it were suggested to you that you might find solace and relaxation by spending the weekend re-hanging the horticultural imple-ments in the pricking-out room, or nailing the shovel to the potting shed wall as it is sometimes termed, but I assure you that a great number of folk spend a good deal of time in quiet and restful contemplation doing just this. I know. There are even television programmes made especially for them. And if I suggested that sliding at maniacal speed down a snow covered precipice was worth doing at a grand a week you'd be dialling the paramedics before I could extol the virtues of lying completely still on a bath-towel for a fortnight wearing nothing but an oily coating of grease and grit and a strategically placed thong thang.

Nope, the fact of the matter is we are all bonkers to a greater or lesser degree, and all that is important really is that we embrace this very diversity of craziness and celebrate it, instead of seeking to grind each and every one of us into a drab conformity of disinterest. Which is the ultimate objective, naturally, of Canneloni Tony and his Cromwellian crew of crawling prodnoses, whose dearest wish is that we should all consent to be moulded in their dull and anodyne image, eating our processed gruel, watching our processed TV, adoring our processed and approved icons and living our sad little processed lives.

So why do I do it? Well, I had thought it was because it permits me to accumulate great quantities of seriously expensive gear, to wear outlandish trousers in polite company without feeling foolish, and go for long walks with some friends, a gun and a sense of purpose, instead of an approved anorak, a fizzy drink and a sense of social injustice. I now realise however that I have been making a political statement which should instantly project me to the cutting edge of libertarian freedom fighting and social acceptability.

In the time that I had been explaining all this to the girl, the pheasants, which had been legging it down the dyke towards the marsh, as Fenland pheasants will, given half a chance and a ditch, met a spaniel coming in the opposite direction which a wily Fenland beater had instructed to "Gerrin yon ditch, an hoofem budsup!", as such beaters do. The pheasants, Fen pheasants never being without a contingency arrangement, therefore adopted Plan B, which was to rise like a jump jet on full thrust, pause for a moment to take a bearing or two, identify which Gun coffee-housing in the distance represented the biggest gap in the line, before making a bee line for the out-door at maximum velocity.

Said Gun, in a flurry of ciggies, matches, flasks and cartridges manages to wrench himself through a knee twisting, braces bursting, disc prolapsing 180-degree turn at the last minute to face himself in the right direction and nails two of the squadron with a right and left which drew enthusiastic applause from the soggy, cold and sceptical girl whom we met at the beginning of this very piece.

Which is, of course, the real reason I do it. The right and left part, I mean. Obviously.

He nearly bit through the stem of his pipe.

Miss Ballantine

I was reading again Georgina Ballantine's description of her epic struggle on the Glendelvine water of the River Tay in 1922 with her record 64lb salmon. It is a piece to which I regularly return. In the absence of being able to catch 64lb salmon myself, or even being able to fish for them on a regular basis, there is nothing for it but to listen to the exploits of others.

In addition to which it does me good to contemplate the sheer effort involved in these ancient battles. Imagine fishing all day with a sixteen foot double handed split cane rod. With two hundred yards of braided horsehair line on a wooden reel the size of a dinner plate and a twenty foot woven silk leader. The weight of the whole set up must have been beyond belief, and as for the feasibility of fighting some great leviathan for several hours on gear of such intrinsic fragility - it just boggles the mind and flabbers the gast.

I cannot but admire too the fortitude of a generation of fishers whose idea of a pair of waders for a brisk day's spring fishing on a roughish river, was a decent layer of goose lard, some well wound puttees, a pair of heavyweight tweed breeches and some stout shoes. The tackle bag shrinks at the very thought.

Still, back to Miss Ballantine. There is a marvellous sentence in her journal entry regarding the big fish. Having made a couple of stout runs, during which Miss B and her father had careered about the river, hopping in and out of the boat and dashed back and forth up and down the bank in order to keep in touch, the fish finally paused and gave some considerable thought to the whole proceedings. "During this time" writes Miss B "the fish remained stationary and sulked."

There's understatement for you. The whole episode took more than two hours from start to finish. The beast was hooked at 6.15 pm as dusk was more or less falling and was finally boated in the dark. The sulking lasted the thick end of thirty minutes.

The point is that I was reminded of the phrase the other day on our own bit of water when I had a fish that sulked. I was fishing with the

Aging Parent, for trout I'm bound to say rather than salmon, and with a normal set up. Which in our lives means a ten foot, three ounce, graphite rod, a floating line in fetching fluorescent pink with a nine foot 3lb nylon leader. I can't tell you what bug was on the end of all this because as I am always explaining I can't remember their damn names. It's not especially important. I think it was a black one.

We were fishing from the sea-wall side of the lake. The wind had been blowing consistently northerly for a week, and the AP's view - he being a bloke who thinks about these things - was that the trouts' food supplies would have been drifting down to the sea-wall end accordingly. Accumulated there would be a fishy buffet of epic proportions, and congregated there too, in his opinion, would be every fish in the district. Of course this also meant that we would be casting into the teeth of said breeze. Which in my case means flailing back and forth half a dozen times, before depositing several yards of line neatly in a heap at my feet; with a fly on top. Still, if it makes the old boy happy. To make matters worse, such weed as floated on the surface had also congregated at the sluice end, so that in order to make any sort of contact with the actual water, we had to cast beyond a twenty foot blanket of the green and gruesome. So there we were. He shooting out his usual thirty yarders and me flailing and spooling as described. Still, the sun shone. Life could be worse.

Then the breeze died. Just like that. Pooooff! Gone. Several flails later and I laid a dead straight cast gossamer light well beyond the weed. Chuffed or what? And having finally got the bait thus far, I savoured the moment and left it there for the nonce. This, I felt, deserved time to be savoured, and a ciggy to boot. So having got lit up and having relished the moment I began to retrieve and to quote Miss Ballantine once more "the bait he seized with no great violence" on about the third tug. After which nothing. No jiggle. No scorching run. Zippo. The Aging Parent, seeing my rod tip bending came bustling up, as APs will. Still nothing moved in the water. "You've caught the bottom" says he, dismissively, "Give it a yank and let's get on." But I was not so sure. I pulled the rod sharply one way, and there was no doubt that the line slowly but surely followed my direction. "Do that again." says he. So I reversed the process, and sure enough the line turned and followed. Whatever was going on, I was not attached to the bottom. I put some more pressure on, fearful of the leader, but gradually the rod unbowed and I reeled in a few feet. There was still no normal response from below however. "During this time the fish sulked." I knew at last what she meant. Again I bent the rod tip almost double, and again I retrieved a few feet. A little easier now. Once I got him moving, it seemed that he went with the flow. I continued the process, feeling as if I was fighting a marlin off Bermuda. My wrist was seriously aching too. Slowly the line cut a path through the weed. I was seriously worried about my nylon with the additional burden, but steady pressure seemed to be doing the trick. Father was fiddling with the landing net.

As the leader knot broke the surface there was a pale flash through the weed. The old man nearly bit through the stem of his pipe. Scepticism forgotten he began to babble instructions as fathers will.

With only a few inches to go the rod tip flew up abruptly and the line slackened and Father blew a series of mains fuses. "Idiot! Nitwit! Cack-hander!" and much else besides. I pointed at the line. The leader was intact. The fly in place. All that remained of the monster was a ribbon of polythene bearing the name of a popular supermarket chain. As the last of the water dribbled out of the plastic bag that I had fought with so resolutely for so long I thought of Miss Ballantine and wondered how she might have reacted if her record Tay salmon, on being gaffed at last, had turned out to be a bin-liner.

I dare say she might have sulked too.

A baton is passed

Future Perfect

I am going to shoot grouse this year. Or at least I am going grouse shooting this year. Many a slip twixt cup and lip and other assorted aphorisms. But all other things being equal I am going to shoot grouse this year. Why is that remarkable? Shooting journos like me spend our lives shooting grouse after all, do we not? Invitations to the finest moors in these islands fall from the Editor's desk like so many ripe fruits in a late summer storm, do they not? They do not.

There was a time when I shot grouse regularly. Not often, but regularly. There were a troop of us in the early days of the Boys' Team (of myth and legend) who used to make the long trek to Scotland at the back end of summer to pursue occasional grouse on the outlying parts of various estates where the older and better heeled guests failed to reach. We yomped and pottered here and there with a motley crew of dogs and girlfriends and from time to time someone would stand on a grouse and it would rocket off, as grouse will when trodden on, and one of us would, might, pot it before it had gone too far. And was there ever such rejoicing over a bird in the bag? I doubt it.

Times though, change; and people with them. Or perhaps not people, but their circumstances. Girlfriends became wives, and with wives came families and with families came responsibilities. And responsibilities came first. And the annual trip north became a snatched weekend; and the team became no more than two or three gathered together for the purpose and finally became just me. And I was no fun. When the dog emigrated into the bargain, it was no fun flat, and I turned to other pursuits in the summer.

For a decade or more I have mustered teams here and there in the winter for a go at the pheasants. It began with day trips and modest outings, by-days of hedges and ditches with perhaps one proper drive after a sandwich and a beer in a barn. Slowly, slowly we graduated to weekends and two days of shooting back to back, and grown up pheasant shooting at that. The team has varied over the years, but not by much,

19

and the only thing which can be said of them with any real certainty is that they have become better and better at it.

In the beginning we always had a couple of duffers in the team. We liked them because they happily chipped into the subscription fund but contributed only slightly to the bag, and that meant more for the rest of us. But they too have got better with the passage of time and now they are, slice them where you will, a pretty fair team of killers. Charming and agreeable and properly discriminating, for sure, but pop a pheasant over, by or round any of them these days within a respectable distance and a pound gets you a penny one of them will top it. There are drives up and down the country where we used to line out in a positive fever of apprehension and were beaten hands down by the keeper and his birds. Now the Boys load up, shrug their shoulders and shoot their socks off.

But of grouse, I haven't seen a feather.

Now an invitation has indeed fallen into my lap. Not a letter now but an e-mail, times change but the content is the same. "We have taken the lodge for a week, so bring rod, stick and gun because we shall be walking the hill, no doubt, and flogging the loch. It's time the kids got their first grouse."

Full circle. The names remain but the faces are, or will be, different. A new generation is poised eagerly to address the hill. Up and down the country, boys and girls – I almost said little; but they aren't any more – even as we speak, are polishing their 28s and 20s and counting their cartridges and trying on stiff new cartridge belts and wondering whether they will come home with grouse and honour.

And do you know the weirdest thing? I shan't mind if I don't shoot a grouse. I shall pack my little 28b to be sure and cartridges too, and if we don't shoot some grouse I will be beside myself; but if I can lend the little gun to someone to shoot their first grouse with, that will be all the pleasure I need. Sitting in the sun on a heather clad hill with a dog and a piece and a grouse or two in the bag, by whomever's hand and aim, will be enough for me. A baton has passed. And it's up to us to make sure it passes again.

Mark you, I'll have the gun back quick enough if the kid misses more than once. Generous and avuncular I may be, but I don't get enough invitations to be that magnanimous and I'm not so old as to be actually stupid. Oh, it's going to be glorious.

Ignorant, wholly unjustified and plain rude.

The Eternal Optimist (Part I)

In the end I had to borrow most of the gear from my brother-in-law.
He has two of everything. I did find my waders however so it wasn't a
complete scrounge, but the Tweed is, when all is said and done, a serious
river and does call for the right tackle. Thus it was that I set off for the
station filled with boyish hope and expectation and laden with as many
bags as a chap can handle. Plus a rod case with little wheels at one end
so that I could drag it along the platform.

I travel a good deal on trains and they really aren't designed
for the peripatetic sportsman these days. There isn't a specific luggage
limit as such, but if you are travelling with more than a carrier bag and
a holdall, then generally speaking you are, in the words of the immortal
bard, stuffed. In the end I abandoned the waders and the rod case at one
end of the carriage and the suitcase and the tackle bag at the other and
slumped into my seat clutching the backpack. Then, because I could not
see the rods and waders anymore because I was facing the wrong direction, I lugged the rod case and the boot bag to the other end and parked
them again, so that I could make sure that no one interfered with them.
I don't suppose that anyone would, but how would you feel if you arrived
for a week's posh fishing in Berwick and your rods got off at Darlington?
Come to that, how would I explain to the b-in-l that his rods had gone
AWOL en route? Call me alarmist, but these things do happen. They
happen to me anyway.

The change at Peterborough was managed without incident and
I found my friend Jonathan hunched over his lap-top beyond the buffet.
I left him to it and settled down with the crossword.

A car and driver were waiting for us at Berwick; Jonathan being
that sort of bloke, and accordingly we were at the St Ednam's House
Hotel shortly thereafter. Was ever a hotel so completely fish-oriented?
My room looked out over the Junction Pool; one of the most famous
sights in the world. To us. Taj Mahal? Tschah! Tour Eiffel? Pah! Junction
Pool? Gosh! Wow! The hall was full of rods and the bar was full of

...filled with boyish hope.

anglers. Principal amongst whom, broadcasting malt with expansive gestures and setting fire to himself with smokes as usual, was the Editor of *Trout & Salmon*. He nearly swallowed his tab and nose-jobbed the malt when he saw me walk in, but soon recovered enough to enquire, in his bluff cheery way, what the dickens I was doing there.

"I'm here to catch a salmon," I said. "I hope," I added. "Have a drink," he said. "And meet the boys and girls," he added. The evening began to dissolve into an agreeable blur of drink and fishing talk..

I did carry away important information however. The river was in fine fettle. The water was nigh-on perfect. There were fish in abundance, though only a few were fresh, the beat I was to fish was prime, they'd had nine in the first two days of the week and even I therefore was in with a decent chance.

At 8.30am there is a migration from the hotel to the tackle shop across the road. As surely as salmon swim upstream a tweedy column snakes its way across the street to replenish lines and lures and to secure the killer flea of the day. A quick computation of the fish reported caught in the bar last night, times the fly they were taken on, divided by the distance from where they were caught to your beat, less the number of pints you and the person you were talking to have had leads you to the Eternal Optimist which is a sort of black and yellow tube and a Gordy Dunn which isn't, but since he is gillying for us we had better have lots. Having spent the GDP of a small country, the tweedy tide rolls back to the hotel and saddles up, and in a scene reminiscent of the start at Le Mans, each team grabs its lunch box from the hall table, legs it to the nearest Range Rover and roars off in pursuit of fish.

We grabbed, we roared, we arrived at the river at a collected canter where the formidable Mr Dunn and his assistant Lee were waiting.

"Ye're hie a' last then?" says he. "And what flee will ye be hurlin' a' ma fush the dee?" We proudly displayed the morning harvest from the tackle shop. "Tscah! No. No. They'll never catch the noo. The watter's too chill. Ye'll be wantin' yin o' thee. Hev ye no gottny? Tach! Whut sort o' fushermen are yu? Ah weel. Ah've a few in ma pock fur ye, anyways.

Just as well one of us kens wha' he's aboot. Let's be at it then. Fush is waitin'."

As if to underline the point a large fish jumped even as the great man spoke. We duly shouldered our rods and addressed the river.

Did I catch one? If you think I'm going to jump to the last chapter at this juncture, you've got another think coming. This is fishing remember: no instant gratification here. A deal of work before you get a sniff. Although Roger, who was another guest in the party this morning, was into a fish before he'd even got his waders wet.

It makes you weep, doesn't it?

Wallflowers at the Ball (Part II)

Now the beat is a beat of three rods and four turns in the river along the way. This means that each fisherman fishes in glorious isolation unseen by the others. So your companions can't see you flailing away and getting your fly caught in the grass at your back or cracking it off on the stones or getting it stuck on the bottom for that matter. It also means that you cannot see how the others are doing and keeps the unhealthy air of competition out of what is, after all, a deeply spiritual and elevating experience.

Until, that is, Gordy puts in an appearance. "Hev ye no catched a fush then?" he roars from the opposite bank. "Not yet," we say, smiling bravely through the disappointment "but it's all in the lap of the gods." "Gods iss it, ye say? Gods be damned! Roger's hed anither agin and the big man's hed two the dee alraddy. Mind, he's a jammy sod. He's as like to catch a fush on his back cast as in front o' yin. I dinna ken hoo 'e

26

duzzit, Ah dinna. Mark you, they're black as ma boots and uglier then ye are, just. Girt lang things, thee are. Tscach! Ye've no a touch, then?" Not even that, we admit. "Tscach!" he says again, "Ah'd best away back then. Yin's probably choking anither as we gas, and he'll like to drown it, wi his luck, if Ah'm no there ta stup 'um."

So Jonathan and I returned to the water with renewed vigour. We waded a little deeper and taking turn and turn about we fished a little harder and a little more diligently and we covered that river inch by inch. There were fish there, no error. We knew that because they kept leaping out of the water all around us, but of takes, snatches, tugs, pulls, knocks and lippings we had not a single tittle, iota or jot.

Lunch came and went. The others were quietly content with their morning's work and there was a robust debate about who was going to be buying the drinks this evening. Jonathan and I listened stoically as the argument veered between the biggest fish of the day on the one hand and the most fish on the other. Jonathan sucked on his Scotch egg and kept his counsel, but I could see that he was prey, as they say, to emotions. I've told you, I know, that he's a successful bloke. And you don't get to be successful, at least not to anything like the extent that he has, by sitting quietly by and letting other people tell you how successful they are. You get off the proverbial sit-upon and get involved and I could see the man's resolution firming up even as we sat there.

We all know, of course, that salmon fishing is pure luck. The fish do not feed in freshwater and their taking a lure in the river is all a matter of irritation, ennui and erratic behaviour. The frightful pheremone means that girls catch all the best fish at the least likely times, but that is science and as fishermen we naturally discard the boffins' conclusions out of hand altogether. It is however the case that the harder you work the luckier you get, as the great red bearded gillie never ceases to tell me, and that afternoon Jonathan was working very hard indeed. If we had covered the water inch by inch in the morning he went at it in the afternoon with a microscope. There wasn't the width of a fag paper between casts. And was he rewarded for his diligence in due season?

Was he buggery. In your dreams. Darkness came and with it

came Gordy. "Aye, it's time we were leaving them too't the dee. Hev' ye catched yit? They've hed two more oot the other end, ye ken. Wha, nuthin? Hev' ye bin fushin' or gassing like a lot of wimmin?" and more besides. Jonathan was wearing a face like thunder. Slightly knackered thunder, to be sure, but thunderous for all that.

Talk in the bar that night was all of the day's bags. They'd had 27 out of the Junction. Downstream they'd had a dozen. Our team had seven for the day. Even the Editor and his party had caught fish, and big fish too, 20lbs plus and there were smiles and malts all round and many a bumper of claret was swilled that night, I can tell you. Jonathan and I were the wallflowers at the ball.

We would be fishing separately on the morrow and since one of the ferrules had fallen off the bro-in-law's rod – probably through exhaustion – I was short of a rod for the final day. Given the Editor's expansive mood, fished up and malted up and clareted up as he was, I wondered if he had a spare stick for a struggling scrivener? "By all means," he roared genially, thrusting a glass into my hand, "I've got a nice little 16' graphite Sage sitting in my room. Take it with my blessing. It needs an outing. It's brand new. Never been kissed. Have another?"

Thus it was, dear reader, that the next day found me equipped with the last word in modern piscatorial equipment, confronting the river, by myself, several fish behind the curve and determined that today would be the day.

"Hev' ye a new pole the dee, then?" says Gordy. "Aye weel, it'll do as well as any, Ah s'pose. Hev' ye a flee with ut? Ach, no, no, no. Tha'll niver do the dee. Watter's too clear. Ah hev' the very thing hiar. Aye, tha'll catch; happen it's in the reet place. Let's gie t'oot then. Tight lines."

Was I going to end the year with a fish?

Testing the Mettle (Part III)

The last thing Lee said to me before abandoning me to my own devices was "It's much easier to fish this stretch well, if you cast left handed." Well, thanks for that. If I could shoot out a halfway decent line right-handed, would I still be a salmon virgin at my advanced age? If I could Spey right and left, if I could roll, if I could cast into wind, upstream, over water would I still have blank spaces on the study wall where the modest collection of portmanteau fish should be? If I could cast at all, would I be fishless at forty? Lefthanded forsooth. I'm as likely to have my lure swiped by a low flying pig on the backcast as I am to cast lefthanded without ending up in Kelso A&E with a triple Optimist in my lug.

I had, of course, been thinking the exact same thing myself and duly dismissed the whole concept out of hand as being impossible. Half an hour of flailing away right-handed however convinced me that there was virtue in experimentation and with my heart in my mouth and both eyes firmly closed against the inevitable, I changed hands, heaved and flung.

Immediately the line went taut. I opened my eyes to see in the distance my fly winking at me from a bush on the far bank. It is a testament to modern technology that given even half a chance your Kevlar-graphite-space-age-lightasafeather-super-rod will, notwithstanding the rank incompetent on the thick end, nonetheless hurl a lure further than anyone might reasonably expect. And the cute Sage that the Editor had loaned me was no exception. I gave the flea a bit of a yank and it duly fell into the stream and floated off as fleas are supposed to, given a decent chance. Brimming with new-found confidence therefore and quite suddenly casting better left-handed than ever I have right, I fished the pool down without incident and wondered what to do next.

"Hev ye took owt then?" came the roar from the bank. "Ye man's had 'us fust, ye ken. And 'us second for the matter of tha'. I dinna doot he's inna 'us thud be noo. Yin's like a bishop in a bordello, wi'a grin ye couldn'a gie off wi' a chisel. Ye've no had a touch then?" I shook my

I don't think the buddha was a fisherman.

head. "Fish 'er doon agin then. It's your turn mind."

So I did, and then I plodded back up the bank to the hut for lunch. Gordy was right about one thing. You couldn't have got the smile off Jonathan's face with anything short of surgery. After a score or more years of drought, he had finally cracked it. And how. He'd caught his first fish at about 11.00am; a nice fresh eight-pounder. On the basis that when one fish takes, others might also be in the mood, he was herded back into the river before he had finished giving proper thanks and capering about the bank, whereupon he promptly caught another one. Not content with that he had caught two more before midday and was in the process of returning his fifth of the morning as I arrived at the scene of the disaster. Whereupon, naturally, he proceeded to explain to me, in very considerable detail, exactly what the answer was and exactly where he had been going wrong all these seasons past, and exactly how I should get on and do the same. I smiled and nodded and ate sausage rolls and tried not to burst into tears.

Now here's a thing. He caught two more during the course of the afternoon, so he had gone from being a salmon fisherman who had never caught a salmon to being a salmon fisherman who banks a fish an hour in the course of a single session. The true horror of the situation didn't dawn on him until later when it struck with the force of a runaway emotional freight-train. Somewhere about the middle of the malt bottle, while he was explaining why he had let his cast come round just a little more because some instinct told him that another fish would hit if he did. Seven fish in the day. Outside of the Ponoi the likelihood of doing that again, or of beating his own record, is zip. Zilch. Nada. Several lotteries-worth to one. Seven is a life changer. You can never go back. Two or three in a spell means nothing to the man who catches seven in a day. Four in a morning is pedestrian stuff to the seven a day man. Half a dozen don't get the pulse racing. There are still very big fish to catch, of course, 30lbs plus would give you something to talk about in the bar, but until then, you are stuck with the "Seven Fish in the Day" story. Probably forever. He left for the airport a broken man.

I, on the other hand, was the only member of the party now still

31

fishless. Clearly something had to be done.

"Give me a fresh fly and a bit of a space, Gordy," says I "it's high time I got in on this act." "There's yer flee and there's yer watter, mon," says he. "And now you've a mind to catch fush, ye'd best get a' it."

With steely determination, I strode into the river. With renewed vigour, and left-handed to boot, I cast out my lure. With implacable inevitability I felt the fly thump into the small of my back.

Was it Confucius or the Buddha who said "The destinies of no two men are the same." I think it was Confucius. I don't think the Buddha was a fisherman.

Thou Shalt not Covet (Part IV)

I was in something of a mood as I walked back downstream, I can tell you. Part of me just wanted to kick the rock at the sheer bloody injustice of it all. Jonathan, fishing with my gear, or more properly with my bro-in-law's gear, but which I had borrowed for him, casting adequately but hardly stylishly or with any distinguishable verve or brio, in a pool which I had fished down earlier in the day and with the same fly, has five salmon in the course of the morning. I hadn't so much as a pull. Where was the fairness? What was the point? What had I done so wrong in my life that he hadn't done worse in his? I respect the river and the fish. Do I curse and swear? Certainly I do but not at or in front of the fish. I drink. I smoke and where and when the possibility presents itself which it does about as often as a buckshee week on the Tweed, I fornicate. So do a lot of people and they all catch more salmon than I do. So just what is the issue?

The other part of me naturally was offering up any sort of simple fisherman's prayer.

...you know, Lord, size doesn't matter.

"Oh Lord, please grant my fervent wish,
that some time soon I catch a fish.
A pound or two, or even fatter,
you know, Lord, size doesn't matter."

And all the other verses into the bargain.

Now after lunch I was on the bottom of the beat. I was all on my own because the other two rods are either boat borne, at least for some of the time, and anyway I was very much the junior partner on this outing and so I got last bite at the staff, as it were.

I had however been told very firmly what I was to do. "Gie yersel' gey inta th' river and stood on the shingle bank tha' runs doon th' mittle of th' stream, ye ken? Then fush 'er doon tae th' carner and beyond. Dinna whate'er ye do step forwards or backwards off the shingle or ye'll be awa' wi' th' watter. An' if ye gie in, walk 'im back up stream, gie oot an' hoick 'im ower the shingle and kill 'im i' the slack. Ye'll be fine. Aye."

So there you have it. Have you ever come across Inner Game Theory? I remember some American expostulating it on the telly once. It impressed me mightily. It is a sort of slacker's charter. Knowing full well what is expected of you under any and all sporting circumstances, you ignore everything in the book and simply go with the flow. You know those amazing cross court returns that you knock off during a tennis warm up that are never to be repeated during a game? Or the perfect drop-kick that sails between the uprights almost from the half-way line when no one is watching? That's Inner Game Theory, that is. Let the concentration wander for a moment and natural, or in my case wholly unnatural, genius bursts forth of its own accord.

So I waded out onto the shingle bank, as ordered, and began to fish down towards the corner. Nothing happened. I was Saged up and casting like a god. Thinking of nothing in particular, leaning on my stick and letting the fly come round entirely of its own accord. Smoking de temps en temp. Nothing. The light began to fade. I was almost down to

34

the corner and dark thoughts of another blank were bubbling uneasily away in the back of my mind. Then the fly stopped. "Shingle," I thought, "Let it sink too far." So I raised the tip of the rod and gave it a bit of a yank. Nothing happened. "Weed," I thought. "I'll have to walk down a bit and try to poke it out with the stick." I took a couple of steps downstream and the fly moved a couple of steps with me. I took another step and the rod tip was abruptly yanked downwards and the reel whined as line was stripped from it, under pressure.

"OHMYGOD!OHMYHEAVENS!IT'SAFISH. WHATSHALLIDO!" I thought. The wise words came back to me. "Walk 'im back up stream, gie oot an' hoick 'im ower the shingle and kill 'im i' the slack."

So I kept the tip up, tightened the brake on the reel and began to walk none too steadily backwards the way I had come.

"PLEASEDON'TGO!PLEASEDON'TBREAK!OH,PLEASE, PLEASE!" The rod was bucking in my hand as I felt my way upstream and started across towards the bank. All I had to do now was to "hoick 'im across the shingle". So I put a bit of pressure on and lowered the rod in the required direction. After a few more jolts the fish and I were reunited on the same side of the gravel bank. I stole a look at my watch. Five to five. With any luck Gordy would be along in a minute or two to pack me up for the night. Just hold on for a few more minutes. "JUSTAFEWMINUTES!" The fish and I were in something of a stalemate. I had no means of landing him and he seemed disinclined to go anywhere much. He went round in circles in the slack water and I watched him do it. Aeons passed. The fish circled. I watched.

Then a voice said "Ye can pull 'im up the stains any time noo. Ye've near drooned the puir wee thing." So I walked back a few steps and pulled and Gordy got a hand in his gills and a handsome silver 12 pounder lay gasping its last on the bank.

"Aye weel," says Gordy, "I suppose noo ye'll be callin' yersel' a fisherman."

Damn right I am.

Advice for beginners

Well, the best time to start the young, or even the not-so-young - let's call them the inexperienced - is after Christmas - Boxing Day for choice actually. So here is the definitive Roderick's advice to the inexperienced, of whatever age.

First and foremost remember that shooting is not a cheap undertaking. If you have paid for your own, this will be a fact well known to you already. I don't wish to harp on about the subject of money, for that is not the point. The point is that you and your fellow Guns have been mustered, it is important that everyone recognises either the generosity of one's host - if a guest - or the fact that one's fellow Gun's have stumped a goodish wedge of their own to be present.

It is crucial therefore, given the sundry contributions that have been invested in the day, both material and emotional, that everybody has a good time. And that means geniality of atmosphere. And that means being nice to everyone. And that, most importantly, involves not shooting them. Nothing spoils a Gun's enjoyment of a day out more than being shot. So then, safety comes top of everybody's list of politenesses. I shall not weary you with the list of how to be safe: get a book. Broadly speaking I recall what the RSM said at school. "Never," said the RSM, "point your gun at anything you don't intend to kill." Of course, he said "rifle"; but the point is well made and covers the ground just handsome in my view. Shooting people is very rude. Rule One: Don't be rude to the Guns. And that goes for hosts and beaters and pickers up and - well, everybody really. And their dog.

It is also important to remember that the keeper has been working all season, all summer, all year, all his life - yea even unto the umpteenth generation - and well into the dark forsooth, in order to put the odd bird over your head or in your way. He has hatched them, nurtured them, fed and watered them. He has fed them out, dogged them in, chased them roundabout - all for your momentary pleasure. Don't therefore under any circumstances be dismissive of the birds. If they fail utterly to perform in any kind of approved style, do not proclaim your disappointment loudly and bruit it about. First because it is only your opinion, and the other Guns may, for all you know, be thinking that this is the bee's proverbials bird-wise, and you will look like a total poseur if you sneer at them. In addition to which it is none of your damn business, but a matter between your host and his keeper. If you are disappointed, upbraid the host - not his staff. Tipping the keeper is a matter for your own judgement. But remember this: a keeper who rears and releases 50,000 head of game on steeply sloping country has no difficulty rounding up a couple of hundred for your delectation. A keeper who finds you two or three score and shows them to advantage on unpromising ground is worth a sight more in my book. I tip the effort not its effect. Rule Two: Never disrespect the keeper.

More particularly, when the birds have done the decent and flown high, wide and handsome, show them especially the respect they deserve. Do not sleeve your gun at the end of a staggering drive and simply walk from your peg. Unless you have failed to connect with anything whatever, in which case you should stay anyway; probably on your knees. Collect your birds, or supervise their collection by pickers up. Do not throw them in a heap either. It makes my blood boil to see the callous disregard with which some Guns treat their game. These birds died for you. They were not mere targets. Never toss them on the ground as if you do not give a monkey's. You'll never be invited again. Lay them by your peg neatly; salute them for the pleasure they brought you and then leave. One day you may find yourself shooting big game, and if you have no respect for your quarry it will bite you in the arse. And rightly so. Rule Three: Never diss the quarry.

Finally - enjoy yourself. It is what you are there for after all. Relax. Select your birds, shoot them, have a good time. There is no point in ignoring all the modest birds and missing all the highest ones and having a generally miserable outing. Don't think that because your neighbours are slotting soaring archangels left and right that you have to as well. That's it. My advice to novice Guns.

All I Want For Christmas

A pair of Purdeys finest would seem to be the logical choice, or better still a garniture. Just imagine waking up on Christmas morning and seeing the brassy corner of that particular parcel poking from the stocking at the end of the bed. But would they be practical? Aye, there's the rub. What would I do with a pair of Purdeys? They do tend to impose somewhat on your lifestyle, rather like driving a Lamborghini, or a Rolls.

You have to be able to use them to devastating effect, for a start. "See the Gun at yonder peg," the beaters murmur to one another "that's a Purdey he's got there. Saw it in the trailer. He'll be a bit useful, eh?"

Well maybe so; on those days when the smile of the good Lord falls upon me and I can thin out elements of His Creation with the best of them. But what of the other days, when I foozle the simple partridge and deliver limping pheasants into the arms of the waiting pickers up?

"See yon Gun with the Purdey," say the beaters then "all the tackle and scarce the nouse to point the right end. It's a crying shame. Shouldn't be allowed out," and more besides. A reputation for meanness follows hot on the heels of he who inadvertently acquires such luxuries. "See yon Gun with the Purdeys," goes the talk: "tipped me a tenner he did, and him with all the cash to shop in Audley Street. He's closer to his wallet than he is to they pheasants, any road up." Oh, it's a hard path to tread when once you place your feet on the soft road. Not that it does your social standing much good either.

A leading colour glossy magazine for today's woman advised its readers recently not to associate themselves with gentlemen, if they can be so described, who drove a particularly glossy brand of sportscar much associated with the young and, at any rate (usually very fast), mobile. "Avoid such men," the mag intoned. "The chances are that the car is all he has."

It went on to suggest some fairly unsavoury, and sketchily researched, comparisons between the performance of the motor in question and the adequacy of the driver under very different circumstances. On the assumption that the analysis is able to be extended thus far, the prospects of one's accoutrements in the field leading to a chance to exercise one's swing in the butts of the boudoir seem remote indeed. A pair of Purdey's does not necessarily make difficult birds easier, it just looks that way.

One also has to consider the impact of one's request on dear old Santa himself. "The little perisher wants a p-p-pair of P-P-Purdey's!!!" Imagine the consequences of such an expostulation while munching on one of Mrs Santa's mince pies. Shards of pastry would be ricocheting off the walls of the Claus igloo like shrapnel, probably adding a number of elfin workers to the game sleigh in the process, and then where would we be?

Snowball

And then there was Snowball. Actually he was called Snowy, although no one could remember quite why. Blackie Cole, Tiddler Lane, Cobbler Parr all had logical derivations. Even Cuckoo could imitate a cuckoo well enough, when he remembered to put his teeth in, to justify his nickname; but Snowball made no sense at all.

He always said, in those moments of lucidity of an evening that came between the last pint that he would remember and the first that really counted, that the nickname had to do with his real name, which he had changed when he ran away from the circus.

Now most people in my experience, and there have not been many I have to admit, who undertake serious lifestyle changes, run away to join the circus. Indeed, I would wager that most stories along these

…three days' stubble and no teeth.

42

lines tend in that direction. Snowy did the reverse. History never related what he was doing with the circus in the first place and whether there was an early chapter that we never did get to the bottom of. Howsoever it came about, when the circus arrived in the village, Snowball was with it, and when it left several days later, he wasn't.

This would have been between the wars, mark you, and nearer the first than the second for that matter. Anyoldhow, Snowball got a job on one the farms as a horse man. Which conjures up visions of great Suffolk Punches and Shires curvetting and pirouetting their way along the furrows before the plough while Snowball stands balanced on their rumps cracking his whip and bowing to an audience remembered.

By the time I knew him, of course, he was long since retired but still lived in the same cottage which he had been granted when first he had sought work on the estate. Nor had it much changed in that time. He had adopted the electric light, I recall, but still did his cooking on the range – and did such bathing as he ever did on the rug before it – and he wouldn't have an inside loo for love nor money. Have a thing like that in the house? Disgusting.

He filled his days bicycling very slowly around the village and its environs, largely from pub to pub with his gun slung under the cross-bar and his game bag slung across his shoulder. And during the summer hols I would mooch with him.

He always used to whittle a stick while he walked. He only had a modest little penknife, but he would pick out a decent staff as we passed a hedge after breakfast and as we walked he would trim it up and whittle away at it, until there was a smooth knob at one end that settled easily into the hand or under the armpit with equal facility.

I could tell you how he taught me to walk slowly past the pigeons in the tree and then turn back and shoot them as they clattered out. But that was not a tip; that was because Snowball couldn't see very well and used generally speaking to shoot in the direction of the clatter in the vague hope of accidental connection.

It was just as well that Snowball's peregrinations did not bring him into contact with the many ramblers and dog walkers whom one encounters today in the countryside. Basically, if it moved along the ground it was a rabbit, unless it was white in which case it was a sheep. If it flew over his head it was a bird and that was that. Snowball though was an easily recognised character and, of course, if you stood really still as he passed, you could safely be a tree. So unless he tried to whittle your leg, you could remain safe for the time being. The farmer's wife waved to him once as he passed through the kitchen garden once, and came close to paying the price. He never shared with me what game he thought might be in the kitchen garden that was five feet tall, mostly pink and waving at one end, and to be honest, I never had the nerve to ask.

He didn't teach me to shoot really. What he did teach me was how to call a hare. You purse your lips as if for a kiss and then draw in air, also as if for a kiss; and what emerges is a squeak. Just like kissing really, which is probably why hares are forever turning into beautiful girls in stories, or witches and vampires for that matter once they have young men clasped in their arms and glued to their faces, but that's another issue. Then squeaking away like mad you approach the hare, which is rooted to the spot with a startled expression on its face – as you can readily understand at this stage – and as you approach slowly, slowly, with each step you crouch down a little. Such that from the hare's point of view, as you get closer, yet you do not loom any bigger. So the hare stays put. To the point where when you arrive – as it might be, whisker to whisker – and she is about to turn into the beautiful girl as aforesaid and the real kissing is about to begin, and you grab the hare and stick it in your gamebag and leg it off home or back to where we left the bicycles by the hedge. S'Peasy.

Now I only saw Snowy do this the once, but he really did get quite close. He was old as the hills then and if you had seen Snowball, with his bottle-bottom glasses, three day stubble and no teeth all puckered up and advancing upon you squeaking, I dare say you would have been rooted to the spot too. Anyway, the old hare hung about until Snowball was a yard or so off and was hunkered down real small and then she squirted off and was under the gate before you could say "Puss". I watched the old man for several minutes but he just stayed crouched

44

down as if the old hare was still in front of him. I guessed that he was so blind he hadn't seen her push off and was probably in the process of seeking to seduce a clod of plough or an old swede or something and I went over to disabuse him.

I put a hand gently on Snowy's shoulder. "She's gone, old friend," I said helpfully.

"I knows she's ruddy gawn, boy," he says, "An' so's my blasted back. I's bin stuck here five minutes waiting for you to get off yer erse and fetch me up, ye daft beggar."
Still, I thought, as Snowy leaned heavily on my shoulder across the field to the bikes, you learn something new every day.

Flinging, Swishing & Flailing

There was an incident with a sheep a few years ago. However we start, I'm afraid, with the bad news. The RSPCA's somewhat controversially elected Director General Jackie Ballard has announced her distaste for fishing. "It's cruel," she says "to stick a hook in a fish's jaw and then fling it back." Ms Ballard dislikes all forms of hunting for sport. She famously miffed her constituents in the West Country when she was, briefly, their MP, by announcing her disapproval of stag-hunting. Now she has broadened her arc of fire to include game shooting and fishing. She specified coarse fishing in her comments, though why she should I have no idea for I rather doubt she appreciates the fine differences between one branch of angling and another, I suspect she thinks us all equally coarse, and as the consequence we must all consider our positions with reference to the body of which she is principal.

I think her comments are disgraceful. It is very easy, of course, to give the impression of being a really gung-ho and dynamic manager by making broad and sweeping statements and generally declaring war on everybody and everything. "I'm going to change the world!" "I'm going to eradicate badness!" "I'm going to make everything pink and fluffy!" "Everything will be free and everyone will be happy!" "Just send me the money and everything will be all right!" These are easy statements to make. These are a classic substitution of movement for action.

The irony is that the RSPCA really needs the cash right now. Stung by declining revenues and falling stockmarkets at a time when costs continue inexorably to rise, the RSPCA's accounts make sorry reading. The new DG, who by her own admission has little administrative experience and no financial acumen whatever, needs big bucks fast and a broad and simple mission statement to boot. Everyone knows that wars need money – just ask the Chancellor, why don't you? - so a crusade is as good a way of getting into people's ribs as any and requires virtually no detailed explanation. It is a depressing and disturbing development. What really irks me though, over and above being labelled cruel and being attacked by a strident and illiberal and intolerant killjoy, is that phrase "fling it back." That really gets up my nose. I have never flung a fish anywhere. Forwards, back or into a frying pan. Flinging is something you do with something which is of no account. Fling implies no respect. Fling betrays Ms Ballard's utter lack of understanding of the relationship, founded on a proper regard and respect, between a sportsman and his quarry whether it be fur, feather or fin. Fling discards at a stroke the millions of hours and millions more of pounds that anglers spend annually improving and enhancing the habitats of their fish and all the wider conservation benefits which flow from that investment and effort. It is not merely ignorant and wholly unjustified but plain rude and rudeness in a public figure is intolerable. You should all write and tell her.

Deep breath. Move on.

I caught a bat the other night. Not with rod and line but with my landing net. I was dining with friends when there came a squeak or series of alarmed squeaks from their daughter's bedroom. Her Mum went to the rescue and the squeaking doubled. Dad and I, fortified by strong drink, ascended to the squeak zone to find one girl hiding under the duvet and another behind the curtains. Both still squeaking. Also squeaking was the bat which was flittering back and forth in that flittery way that bats do.

A good deal of swishing and flailing.

There is only one thing for it when confronted by such a situation; we went and got some gear. He wanted to use tennis racquets but I pointed out that this was not a sympathetic approach and the girls would be distraught if and when we connected. If we ever did. Bats have this radar thing going, don't they, which means that they don't fly into things in the dark? So how are you going to sock one with a tennis racquet if it doesn't want to be socked? So I went and got the net from the car. Why would a bat fly into a landing net either, you ask, in your relentless pursuit of learning? Well, the fact is that there isn't anything in the opening of a landing net, now is there? That's really the point. The net bit is at the other end. Which is where the bat duly ended up. There was a good deal of swishing and flailing, I admit, before that - and the Postman Pat lampshade will probably never be quite the same again - but once we worked out that just holding the net still was better than taking a proactive pursuit approach to the whole thing, the poor wee bat was soon enmeshed and duly released – or flung, perhaps, if la Bollard ever reads this – outdoors once more, none the worse for its experience.

Father did once catch a bat on the fly. He was fishing a dry Daddy Long-legs and a bat took it on the back cast. I've had a martin once scoop a fly from the surface of the water which was alarming enough but by no means as difficult to remedy as the Canada goose which paddled through a fellow angler's cast on the pond one day. That was a sporting twenty minutes, I can tell you. Why is it that you never have a camera when you need it? It took three of us, one rod and two nets, since you ask, to sort that one out and if there was any flinging being done then it was the goose who was doing it.

There have been any number of waders, jackets, trees, fences, ears, noses, cheeks and jowls, of course, over the years but one tends to take them as part of the territory, and a mate of mine did once catch his own trousers, which he had left on the bank for reasons best not discussed, on the backcast and hurl them into the Tay. I was going to tell you about the sheep, wasn't I? Damn.

Beach Harvest

When you look around, I mean when you really look around, we haven't half mucked the place up. I was sitting on the beach the other day and the nephews returned from a shrimping expedition. "What ho!" says I "and what have we got? Enough to cover a biscuit?" They had scarcely even that. A handful of shrimps, which even if we did the hard hearted thing and took them home to the saucepan wouldn't cover a cracker. "They keep on getting through the net," the tiny anglers argued "and get away." Which was, of course, entirely true; and which is, after all, the purpose of the net in the first place. A modest filament to catch the fat and toothsome and to allow the midgets to get away to grow into something better. But now there was nothing better. And the boys had been fishing for a while. When I was a committed shrimper three decades ago, it took no more than an hour, in a favoured spot mark you, to half fill a bucket with shrimps the size of a finger – albeit a junior finger. Now a morning's toil nets no more than a handful.

In those days shrimps were not the only quarry either. For those with the stomach for it there were mackerel too. A dawn raid on the incoming tide with handlines and some hooks decorated in coloured feathers or shredded tinfoil or both would always bag a breakfast of fresh fish. I didn't do it myself because I get horribly seasick and would spend any such rash outing putting into the seas rather more than I was taking out and not enjoying things a jot, but there were enthusiasts who went regularly and while there were disappointments, they were easily outnumbered by the successes and even the occasional bonanza when the boat would come back almost awash with fish and it was mackerel not just for breakfast and not just for the household but for most of the village as well.

There were occasional shoals of whitebait too. The cry would go out that the whitebait were in and everyone, and I do mean everyone, would scamper down to the harbour with nets and buckets and it was no more or less than a matter of scooping out the little fish at will. I recall

...putting into the sea rather more than I was taking out.

Uncle Peter striding up and down just off the beach, with the water lapping his chest, towing his Guernsey behind him with the sleeves knotted and catching enough for a feast at supper.

Nor was the abundance limited to the tides. We could rake up the cockles after the water had gone or with a fork and a sieve collect a pint or two of "Stiffkey Blues" in little more time than it takes to tell; and that was discarding anything that couldn't cover a half crown piece. The mussel beds were off limits since they were seeded and jealously guarded by the mussel men who were bearded and tough and deeply scary. It was an odd day though when you could not find a string of molluscs hanging from a rock well away from the main beds where an anarchic seed mussel had struck out on its own for a season.

And clams. Running along the sand with a trowel in one hand, sticking fingers down likely looking holes to feel the cold tickle of a rapidly burrowing clam and digging after it like a mad thing.

Or forking the dabs. Striding back and forth across the estuary with the great trident stabbing blindly away at the depths below in the vague hope of connecting with a flattie. Was there ever a time when they were so abundant that there was a snowball's chance of getting one by such a precarious means? The nephews know nothing of these thrills and skills. The mussels went when the last of the mussel men retired. No one in the next generation had the inclination, or the knowledge probably, to scratch such a subsistence living from the shore any more.

The cockles and the clams went in the 70s, I guess, as a combination of pollution on the one hand and the shifting of the sands on the other. Once the harbour shrank as a commercial inlet the groynes and sea-breaks were allowed to deteriorate and the winter storms soon reorganised the sandbars and the flats and that finished whatever shellfish the effluent had left behind.

Of the mackerel and the whitebait and the dabs, the bass and the occasional sea-trout for that matter, I imagine, actually I know – we all know - that the industrial ravaging of the North Sea by commercial fleets has left stocks at the margin or below sustainable levels and the survivors are running the proliferating gauntlet of coastal seals who neither know nor care whether the next fish they eat is the last of its species or not. And now even the shrimps are dwindling by all accounts, or at least by the accounts of boys who have been plying their own modest trade for several seasons now and have learned the difference between the good places and the bad and the importance of keeping only the biggest and always to check to see if they are carrying roe on their bellies because we don't want the shrimping to dry up too.

When you look at it we haven't half mucked the place up. It's time we did something about that.

Trouble with Cats

Let me tell you about the cat issue. Or rather let me put my side of what became known around the village as the Laundry Room Incident. First off I should explain that the laundry room is converted from one of the outhouses. It is the smartest of them. The others are the coal shed and the boat shed, and maintain a becoming primitiveness. The Laundry Room is posher by far, not least in that it has a ceiling. And in the ceiling, wailed my sister who was staying, were rats. "So call the ratcatcher," says I, rational as ever. She duly did, and by the time I got home Len the ratcatcher was leaning a ladder against the wall and prising off one of the tiles for a recce. There was a noise like ripping canvas, a lot of scampering, and Len from pest control was teetering atop his ladder in a style that would have won applause in any three ring circus. As he picked himself up and we dusted him down he explained the difficulty. "Them's not rats," says he, "them's cats. I doesn't do cats."

And nor apparently does anyone else. The RSPCA was enlightening but not helpful. Were they my cats? Well, were they anyone else's cats? Was someone being cruel to them? Was I being cruel to them? Not yet. The Society cannot intervene unless there is cruelty to be stopped. If it hadn't started, they couldn't help. They do not do cats either, at least not feral cats. And feral was clearly what we had. I peeked under the roof tile too, and quite apart from a pong that had my eyes watering and my stomach heaving, the bare fanged spitting monster I encountered not a yard away was as far from the contented moggy being stroked by a doting girly as she nibbles her choccy bar or sips her soup or whatever on the telly as you could dream up. I'm no Attenborough but I knew enough to see that what we were up against was not the domesticated version.

"I don't care what it is," said the sister as I scuttled back down the ladder, "it's leaving today, if not before. I'm not having wild things about with my babies in the garden." Well, she had a point. Not only were there the consequences of a crawling tot coming face to fang with a wild pussy, there was the disease aspect to consider. Neither Len nor

COPPLESTONE

...in a riding mac and oven-gloves.

55

I had exactly examined the brutes, but a cursory glance suggested that they were pretty manky. Oh yes; they. What we had here was a family unit. Mum, auntie and as far as we could tell, four kittens; several weeks old and soon ready to join the happy community of manky cats and form family units of their own.

Len agreed to help me evict them, but as he reiterated, he doesn't do cats. I agreed that if he helped me to collect them, I would see to any doing that was required. So, he armed with the stable broom and torch, and me, in midsummer mark you, in a riding mac and oven gloves clutching a landing net, we blocked off any visible exits and went into the roof space from opposite sides.

Let us not dwell on the pursuit aspects. Let us draw a discreet veil over the scamper, prod and scurry. The mad dashes, the clawing, spitting, stinking, peeing, bundles of fury that we managed after longer than either of us might have wished, to get into the canvas mailbag I had purloined for the purpose. Suffice to say we got five out of six. Mum bailed out through a route we hadn't spotted in a flash but we got the rest. And a sad collection they were too. Eyes gummed up and noses running, cat 'flu symptoms I guess; almost furless with mange and crawling with fleas. Not well nourished either for all we also removed a bin liner full of carrion remains, mostly rabbit and small birds, together with several chicken bones that I suspect came from dustbins around the village, rather than coops. Apparently the feral population is badly affected by feline AIDS too, though how one checks for that I don't know. And I'm not sure I want to.

The stench, as you might imagine was ghastly. We must have scrubbed the area with the strongest disinfectants a dozen times since, but on a warm day the unmistakable odour of unrestrained cat still lingers.

The issue now was what to do with the sack, or more especially, its contents. I rejected several suggestions along the lines that the North Sea was only a few hundred metres distant and they were already in a sack. I don't do cats either. At least not that way.

I was eventually helped out by a local vet who agreed to see to them, so I actually succeeded in shirking the job altogether.

At least I thought I had. However the lady of mature years, who was renting the house next door for her summer hols, and who had incidentally her own Tibbles along for the vacation, took a different view. She urged me late that night to permit Mummy cat who was mewing in the street, back into my roof. When I explained that I would permit no such thing, she declared me cruel beyond words; a view she later expressed in forthright terms to the vicar, the RSPCA, the postmistress and the chairman of the parish council.

I am happy to report that all these dignitaries took a more reasonable view of my actions, once I had explained to each of them in turn what the chain of events had been. The story was getting better and better with each telling though and by the time I had headed it off, I was known about the village to have massacred dozens, nay hundreds, of precious pets in the most awful ways.

Still we have no more feral mogs in our roof, touch wood. My problem now is that when they turn up in someone else's attic, my reputation is such that I have become the village cat-man. So for the record: "I never done cats, and I doesn't do cats. But I knows how."

Cowboy Outfits

So the New Year is upon us and the best of the shooting is still to come. January ushers in the less formal shooting and in my life that means that the bulk of my invitations fall in this month rather than the battues that precede Christmas. The weather is more wintry and the roads therefore more treacherous and the railways are more prone even than usual to seize up on account of a modest frosting on the rails. Accordingly it makes sense to undertake a leisurely journey to somewhere within striking distance of the shoot the day before in order that one can pitch up bright and early and comfortably unstressed at the appropriate hour the following morning; bathed, breakfasted and without a lot of tail-lights dancing before the eyes.

Staying at the house is the obvious answer, but it may be that one is not shooting at a venue that has a house or that one is not as closely acquainted with one's host as to impose oneself overnight; or even that one has been banned from the portals following the incident with the billiards room chandelier last year which still stands out in the memory in inglorious technicolour. Whatever.

So it is to the commodious local hostelry that one repairs betimes. Actually, if there is one thing that can compare to the delights of the shooting day, it must be the pleasure of arriving at some pub or inn the night before knowing that the Guns will be gradually assembling for dinner and low jinks, in anticipation of the shoot to come. As you pull into the car park it is possible to recognise the occasional barouche of one of the mates. The vehicles of most shooting types at this time of year are stained with the honourable scars of journeys here and there about the place in pursuit of sport. The mud and salt of countless miles of motorways and occasional cross-country forays between pegs are fair indications. The dog guard in the back is always a good clue too; and of course the gun racks are a dead giveaway. Not that any of us would leave a gun in one unattended these days, obviously. And the occasional familiar number plate is the clincher.

There's gonna be shootin'.

"Marcus is here then," you think, "and if he's about then his brother can't be far behind. That's Paddy's old truck, so he and Uncle Mike will be propping up the bar already. Who else is on the list?" And already there is the growing realisation that this is going to be a corker. With a deal of uncorking into the bargain.

It's a bit like the boys checking in from the four corners of the globe for a major jewel heist. Or the gunslingers moseying into town for a showdown. "I see Johnny Ringo's in town." "Uhuh. And Butch and Sundance." "They packin'?" "Sure looks that way." "There's gonna be shootin'?" "Uhuh. I reck'n." "Whisky?" "Guess so." All right, so I'm a sad cowboy manqué, but the whole thing doesn't really work if the image is of a bunch of ballet dancers pirouetting into the bar for an impromptu rendering of Swan Lake, now does it?

The simple fact is that one doesn't see enough of one's mates for the rest of the year. Work, business, family commitments, more work, school holidays and all the assorted obligations which are the burdens of growing up mean that one can go from one year's end to another without getting together but an invitation to shoot cuts through them all and cannot be denied. Not only is it a splendidly generous gift in itself, but it brings together friends who would otherwise drift away and that is priceless.

Of course, that chandelier in the billiards room was fairly priceless too which is why we are staying in the pub this time, because the other side-effect of bringing together a bunch of mates who haven't seen enough of each other for a while is a certain amount of claret-fuelled boisterousness which has been known to strain the generosity of certain hosts almost to breaking point. Mark you, there are some hoteliers about the place who watch the arrival of a series of salt and mud-spattered vehicles with a certain amount of trepidation and who move quickly to stick the sweet trolley into the cupboard under the stairs for the time being until the storm has passed. But that is another story altogether, which perhaps I'll share with you one day, if we're spared.

...a certain amount of claret-fuelled boisterousness

Dab-Handed

I like the nephews, generally speaking, but they do have the attention span of a small gnat. Probably it has to do with watching too much children's television which issues forth its presentations in ever decreasingly minute pre-digested bite-sized pieces for their better appreciation by small gnats. Telly McNuggets; with a rich sauce of broadly accented whoops of enthusiasm.

Why do I know this? I know this because if the nephews are watching it, and they are, I am wrestling with the daily avalanche of assorted ghastlinesses from around the world which make up the papers and trying, in the midst of a storm of infantile jokes about beans and their thunderous consequences, to get clue one of the crossword. At which point the nephews lose interest in teenaged presenters dressed as bumblebees and decide they want to go sailing. "Please! Please! Uncle Giles, please! Let's go sailing."

To which the only sensible answer is to explain that the tide has been and gone, there isn't a breath of wind and anyway I have a crossword to finish. Actually to start. And after about thirty seconds of earnest debate concerning these apparently insuperable difficulties I am pulling on the swimmers and trudging off to find the boat anyway and girding up the loins for a long drag down the estuary to where the remains of wind and water might yet be found in the pool by the big sea. "But….." and it is an important "But…." heavily charged with partnership, responsibility and all the history of a seafaring nation where crews stick to their guns no matter what and captains go down with their ships, "…you will have to assist with the drag and if you fail to sail enthusiastically when we

One of Mother Nature's little jokes.

get there, we shall be having words." Of course. No problem. Promise. Promise. Promise.

In a pig's eye. Ten seconds, ten seconds being the attention span of the average gnat, or nephew, from the launch of the venerable dinghy the nephews are building mudslides off the marsh and yours truly is contemplating the long trudge towards the beach.

Actually it is not a disagreeable trudge, as trudges go. There is sun and sand and peewits calling and such like and as the last of the previous evening's overindulgence clears from the brain with the exercise there is even a simple satisfaction to be gained from the whole undertaking.

And then you fall into a hole. One moment you are trudging along contemplating such simple pleasures and the next the ground shears away as surely as if you had walked off a cliff and you are clinging to the front of the venerable dinghy, thrashing madly and spouting a mouthful of seawater like a superannuated whale. It's very disconcerting. Not unlike falling into the orchestra pit as you step forward to launch into some great speech. One of Mother Nature's little jokes. Although it is only the nephews who get to laugh at it.

Only this time it was not just the nephews. For upon surfacing, and concluding a somewhat unscheduled drift across the hole in quo, I saw a bloke sitting in a little boat between the groynes which are the tools which Mother Nature uses to construct her little jokes. And he had a rod in his hand. Nothing complicated; a little spinning rig, fibreglass I imagine; such as you might get from the hardware shop in the village alongside the buckets and spades and kites and windbreaks which make up the British holidaymaker's equipage.

And while I watched he wiped the tears from his whiskery cheek and then his rod gave a thoroughly business-like twitch. All at once he was grimly focused. The shoulders stopped heaving, the smile faded, the watering eyes became clear and gimlety. A fisherman into a fish.

Round and round the boat it went with the bloke reeling now and again until at last the water boiled as the fish surfaced. The bloke slipped a shrimp net under it and hoisted a handsome flatfish aboard. A dab. Not a giant, but there wouldn't be much plate showing round it when it appeared on a supper table later I warrant. And then he unhooked it and dropped it into another shrimp net he had as a keep-net and I could see that he had a goodly haul already.

I was deeply impressed, I can tell you. "What are you using?" I called as I set off once more on my trudge, in the time honoured tradition of a fellow fisherman in the relentless pursuit of the answer to the Great Question. "Baited spoon." says he. "Baited with what?" says I. And do you know, I thought I heard something about beads from a Christmas cracker, but I can't be sure because at that moment I walked off a watery cliff and by the time I had surfaced again, thrashing and spouting, I had drifted too far to hear the answer properly. I could hear him laughing though. And the nephews.

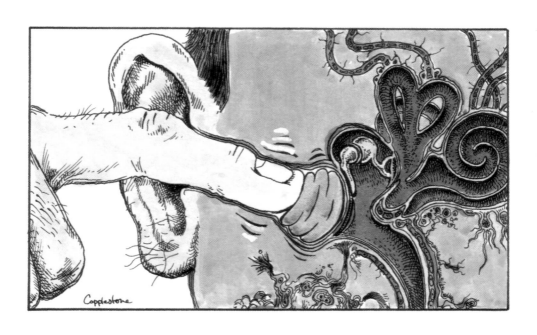

I felt the little blighter all right.

Earplugs

They say that things happen in threes. Well, I hope they are wrong. Because I have got two things dangerously stuck in places and I'm running out of options. I have already told you about the cartridge that went wonky on me and sent the tube part shooting up the barrel to lodge just beyond the chamber. Scary incident number one. I still get goose-bumps just thinking about it.

Not more than a few weeks later I was invited to a simulated game shoot, where the birds are clay and the volume is terrific, and you might easily let off 250 bangs in a day. You know the sort of thing. I have written them up enough times for you, so you should know. Any old how, if you don't, still, I recommend the whole outing as a blast of the highest order and a bargain to boot. The essence of the story though is that this being a summer event, not all of the necessary kit was in the right place on the morning in question.

During the proper shooting season, of course, the shooting gear - in its entirety - is never far from the surface of the house. Guns, cartridges, boots, hat, stick. These are things of key importance on the shooting morning. Guns and bangers are in the safe; stop one. Boots, hat and stick are all assembled by the stand in the hall. Shirts and socks and silks and smalls are clothes and live where all clothes live for the most part, which is either on the floor or in the washing machine. Keys, wallet and earplugs live on the hall table. Except in the summer they don't. At least the earplugs don't. Where they do live I haven't the faintest idea, but on the hall table they ain't.

Now I know that there is a wide variety of ear defences available to the modern sportsperson. These range from your basic foam or even wax plug, which one squishes between the fingers until it is pointy at one end and more or less flat at the other and which is then driven firmly into the lug with the ball of the thumb.

It blots out the noise of shooting for sure; as indeed it blots out all forms of sound transmission whatever. In effect it renders the wearer deaf as the proverbial post. Stoners. Accordingly friends tend to talk about one behind one's back. Indeed to one's face. In fact they eventually lean very close and sort of screw their faces up very strangely and go red and watery eyed as they bawl from the closest range "You can take them out now. We are going to lunch." And you smile and nod and walk off to your peg. Or into a tree; or whatever.

At the other end of the scale are those great muffler affairs that they wear on the wireless and in helicopters. "Nice shooting, Red Leader, that'll win you a case of beers. And now here's a song for Europe." You know the sort of things. They have batteries and knobs and will permit you to listen to a gnat passing wind three fields away but will protect you, at one and the same time, from the blast of your own gun three feet away. Quite apart from hearing a good deal about oneself that one would rather remain ignorant of, when picking up the fag-ends of the conversation from the peg next door ("If the greedy bastard nicks one more of my birds...."), I have always had misgiving about the possible deafening consequences of, say, a cow letting a ripe one go at close range. I mean is that really something one wants to hear? Plus they cost a mint.

In between are the little rubber jobbies, which seem to do a very adequate job while neither breaking the bank nor making me look like a spaceman. Plus they are cheap and this is important as I lose them at regular intervals. And they come in a variety of sizes. Well, small, medium and large. I am a medium. The girls in my life tend to be small - in the ear department anyway. Not that it makes much difference. Or so I thought when I realised at said simulated shoot that I had brought the smalls instead of the mediums. Now a game shoot where one lets off from time to time is a different issue noise-wise from a simulated shoot where hundreds of rounds in a day is not unheard of. Ergo big noise. Ear protection is imperative.

So I bunged in the small plugs and ploughed on. After the first drive I was chatting away so easily with the other Guns that I really wondered if I had ear plugs in at all. I reached up a finger just to check. That was my second mistake. I felt the little blighter all right, slipping down the old tube like a weasel up a drain-pipe. I suppose my third mistake was cramming the rest of my pudgy digit down after it in an effort to retrieve what was now clearly an escapee ear-plug. Eventually my host - a man equipped for every situation - asked me why I was kneeling on the ground, apparently attempting to head-butt the very earth into submission.

I explained quietly, discreetly; and he exploded into roars of laughter and loudly informed everyone of my dilemma. My how they laughed! "Which ear?" says he. And when I told him, he caught me a tremendous clip on the opposite ear. "Has that shifted it, then?" he says helpfully. "Not outwards, at any rate," says I. "Well, we could always push it right through with a cleaning rod" he continues, fingering his knife "or we could operate directly, I suppose."

In the end we managed to extract the blasted thing with a pair of eyebrow tweezers that one of the ladies present had in her vanity case in the car. Which was, I will tell you, as blessed a relief as I can remember, because it was a) quite painful at this point having been forced ever further inwards by a variety of mechanisms; and b) I was beginning to get quite seriously alarmed by the whole situation.

So, shell jammed in gun; plug jammed in lug. As I said I hope things don't happen in threes because there are a limited number of possibilities remaining in my life and none of them are particularly appealing. I may have to engineer the situation to make sure it is not the worst that can happen that happens. Before you are too critical next time you see a bloke in your local casualty department with a saucepan on his bonce, or a section of railings draped about his shoulders, just think it through. He may be rounding out a series.

...deposit the requisite Smarties under the Holy Stone.

Fishing Foibles

There is a charming tradition in Scotland at the commencement of the salmon fishing when the boys and girls assemble on the riverbank to toast the forthcoming season and to offer a libation to the river gods. This is done by sploshing a good deal of malt into the river and a good deal more down themselves. And then some more for good measure. I think it is pretty much a truth universally acknowledged that slopping perfectly good whisky, or as it might be whiskey, into a river is going to do little enough towards anyone catching anything. Not least because most folk won't be in a position to fish until tomorrow or next week or later or when they have sobered up, so that any alluring effect the scotch, or as it might be the whiskey, has on the fish will be at best diluted and at worst where reality meets theory and hope and expectation mingle; which is to say somewhere in mid-Atlantic.

Nonetheless no one who fishes will be inclined to deny the gods their fair share of anything which is going. Nor for that matter the fairies, the little people, the trout goblins, the mayfly maidens, the dancing sedgettes or indeed the tanglies.

It all depends where you are, who you are and the sort of mood that takes you. There is a gillie I know who swears blind that there is no point even approaching the river unless you have deposited the requisite Smarties under the holy stone. And you might as well pack up and go home anyway if they haven't been removed by lunch-time. I'm never really sure whether he is serious about this or whether he is yanking the proverbial. What I do know is that there is a water bailiff in the Home Counties who will write you off as a dedicated no-hoper unless you start the morning by broadcasting wine-gums about the bank.

I suspect that there are elements of truth, or if not truth then at least rationality, about these somewhat bizarre habits. A gillie, for example, has only a little time to size up his guest who may be his responsibility, and to all intents and purposes his employer, for the next day, week, whatever. Now it wouldn't really be on, would it, to ask for

71

guests' references to be sent in advance? But there is nothing that says he can't set a little test on arrival. Test the mettle, so to speak? How badly do you want to catch a fish? Badly, badly. Would you get up early and work the river hard? Yes. Certainly. Would you use the fly I recommend and the pools as I choose? Of course. Of course. Will you do as you are told, where and when, rain or shine? I will. I will. Will you put six orange Smarties under the wee rock yonder? If I have to. Will you dance naked in the moonlight wearing only a pair of waders and a freshly cut thistle? Er, I'm not sure that I would go as far as all that, actually. Well, no Sir, that won't be necessary at all, Sir. Just my little joke.

But you can see how you are already neatly characterised for the duration of your stay. Moderately desperate. Basic manageability. Slavishly obedient, but not completely without scruples. If only most job interviews were so perceptive.

The point is though that we are none of us without our rituals. Most of which are founded in fact. I am of the opinion that in the absence of any kind of fishy activity at the pond, the best thing to do is to stick the rod under one arm and light a ciggy. This usually gets the fish moving. Obviously it does; because they can see that I'm not concentrating and know therefore that there can be no point of connection between me and the lovely juicy, luminescent lure lying just in front of their collective nose. Hence they take and I am back in action. That's my theory anyway.

The truth is actually that in my frustration and excitement I have been casting faster and more furiously with every cast. This means that my presentation of the fly has been shorter, splashier and generally less attractive even than my usual brick-like efforts. As a consequence of which I have hoicked it back in a fury with little or no ceremony whatever in order to hurl it back out with more energy and less effect each time.

When I stop for a ciggy though, I don't cast very hard or very far, because I know that I am going to stop for a ciggy. So the line shoots out for miles and drops gossamer-gently on the surface; just as it should.

Then while I search the many, many, many pockets of the fishing waistcoat for the fags and the matches, and footle about setting fire to my hand, my lapel, my hat and the cigarette in roughly that order, my distant nymph is drifting down through the water to where the fish are, and have been all morning, in the cool depths. And for this cast, at least, my ferocious stripping will not whip it away just as the poor trout are getting interested. Hence they get the chance to take; as indeed do I. Which relaxes me, so I don't thrash to anything like the same extent, which means the fish take more, which means that I catch them, which makes me happy and proves my point that there is nothing like a cigarette to get the fish going.

That's my theory and I'm sticking to it.

The follies of men's youth.

Black Powder

We finally got to do it. And I have to tell you about it because it was just wonderful. We'd been planning it for a year or more and every time we came close something got in the way. But finally it all came together with a whoosh. And a bang. And clouds of smoke. And showers of sparks. And even, from time to time, a terminally disconcerted pheasant. I am talking, as if you hadn't guessed yet, about the black powder experience.

The Boys' Team (of myth and legend) has been contemplating such an outing, as I say. We have been giving a good deal of thought to the big bag issue and we have been turning in our minds ways in which we can manage generally smaller bags with no discernible diminution of fun. We have shot a lot of pheasants over the years and the numbers, I admit, have been creeping upwards rather than down. It is the case however that the small days tend to shine in the memory as much, if not more, than the more prolific outings. Mainly this derives from the sight, which remains etched in the memory, of the Boys *en masse* on hands and knees sneaking up to a hedge in a forlorn attempt to ambush the only pheasant in the county.

Needless to say when they sprang to their feet, guns poised for the shot, the cock in question stood looking at them as if they were mad, which was a forgivable position for him to take, and then stalked slowly but firmly into the ditch at their feet and legged it. He could see they were sportsmen, you see, who would never molest a bird on the ground. He has no idea how lucky he was, and quite possibly remains.

...a bit like watching Trafalgar.

So what we determined to do was to shoot with black powder and see how we got on. As with all Boys' Team decisions this was enthusiastically endorsed, toasted with another bottle and then duly forgotten about. Until Uncle Mike (our oldest member) announced that he'd bought some cartridges. Gamebore load black powder cartridges. Call it a gratuitous plug, I don't care; they make them and Uncle Mike bought them. That's the whole deal. They're pricey, right enough, but when you are coughing three times the going rate for some non-toxic shells, take it from me, the poudre noire comes as a positive relief.

So Uncle Mike had the bullets and the rest of the Boys went and rummaged about in their gun safes and attics and produced a creditable array of elderly hammer guns. And what a joy some of them were. Hollis, Reilly, Grant, Hussey, Hollands, even a thumb-hole Purdey saw the light of day for the first time in donkey's years. Damascus barrels and dragon's head hammers in all directions. There was a moment's concern when we thought that our host might take the hump if he thought we were not treating his pheasants with the seriousness they deserved, or that his beaters' safety might be compromised by us lot careering about with 150 year old shooters - but a quick call confirmed that we would still be welcome. He may have paled at the thought but you can't see that on the telephone, can you?

The day was glorious. Right up on the Norfolk coast. Thick frost crisp on the trees and underfoot; blue sky; sunshine. Not an ideal shooting day, perhaps but beautiful beyond words. A jewel. We lined out and waited.

It was wholly appropriate that Uncle Mike should start proceedings. Cock pheasant came gliding his way, well up and going like the clappers. Mike hefts up, cloud of smoke rolls forth followed by a low roar. Pheasant duly bounces on the plough. Boys cheer. Uncle Mike calls from within the smoke "Did I get it then?" Before anyone can answer more pheasants are in the air and the line is broadly engaged.

What follows was a bit like watching Trafalgar. Clouds of smoke billowing as salvoes are discharged. No bangs but great low roars echoing up and down the valley. With little or no breeze to thin the smoke the line was all but invisible after five minutes, but still the volleys thundered forth. And gales of laughter, a good deal of coughing and spluttering and occasional cheers.

When it was over you never saw a happier team. Smudged, powder stained, tear streaked and still gently smoking they may have been as they emerged, but the experiment was universally deemed, quite literally, a roaring success. For the record, the Boys took on some very spectacular pheasants indeed during the day and managed no less well than with more modern ordnance, as matter of fact. Indeed such is the need with the black powder to give much more lead than with modern propellants that a number of the bag, I would say, were killed more cleanly – and certainly more spectacularly – than usual.

I recommend it unreservedly. We all do. So much so that next season we are thinking of making it compulsory. We might change our name to the Roaring Boys' Team. Or the Hammers, I suppose. Or Heavy Smokers. Or...

Fishing and Girls

Let's talk about girls. I know that in this climate of equality and fair shares for all, we are not supposed to, but these little essays I write are not about Life, the Universe and great Issues of the Day. They are about my experiences, such as they are, and what I, and perhaps you, can derive from them. Anyway, I like talking about girls.

First let it be said that I know all about the Fateful Pheremone. I know that women, as fishers, catch more and bigger salmon than do their male counterparts. I know that if a woman trails her hand in the water where salmon are lying they will do all but nuzzle her fingers. Whereas if a bloke puts so much as a fingertip in the foam, every salmon for miles turns tail and skedaddles directly into the distance. I know all this stuff. During the spate season of the pheremone phenomenon, fishermen of my acquaintance, generally sound and sensible men, to the extent that anyone who stands waist deep in freezing rivers dangling feathers in front of fish and paying good money for the right to do so can ever be called entirely all there, were sneaking elements of the spousal lingerie to keep in their fly-boxes. The more determined, or less rational, whichever way you look at these things, went further, and began to address the women-folk of their acquaintance with fly tying equipment in one hand and scissors in the other.

And much good it did them too. Except that in one notable instance it re-kindled into a flame, yea a furnace, certain passions that had been dormant for a while. Mark you, I'm far from certain that he wouldn't have rather caught a salmon. So much for science.

No, what I want to discuss is the use of fishing as a gauge, a calibration if you like, of the suitability of an individual for the role of mate. There are a number of hurdles which stand in the way of any love affair, and it must be said that fishing is most of them. It is purposeless, even dangerous, to allow fishing to come between people. If you consider that the Highlands in summer cannot be bettered - and you are right - but she believes that Antiguan beaches and a good thick book, or more properly a thick bad book, is the next best thing to Heaven, then, my friend, your passion is set to be cruelly sundered. And you will be spending a good deal of the time apart into the bargain.

Now girls don't have to fish themselves. Indeed there are those who would say that it is a positive disadvantage in a relationship that both parties should pursue the same goals. There is the possibility of unhealthy competition creeping into the affair; and given the higher-than-average performances of notable fisherwomen there are no prizes for guessing who will come second. But they should enjoy fishing. They should have an appreciation of the skills and sciences involved in selecting tackle and using it effectively. They must enjoy the sounds and sights of the rivers, lakes and streams wherein we pursue our quarry. And most importantly of all they should be able to share with the fisherman the excitement of triumphs and the despair of disasters.

I set out these modest requirements not as demands, but as advice. No liaison can survive if the pleasures of the one are squandered on the other, and vice versa. But the most damaging condition of all is indifference. For the man who banks a fresh-run springer to be met with "That's nice, dear," disaster looms. Not to mention the possibility of a stiff sentence. Though if the judge is a fisherman, he may knock it back to justifiable homicide. If when advice is sought on likely flies for a given water, there comes the suggestion of "One of the pretty blue ones," one can say with certainty that this relationship will not last. And the beloved who is off catching dragon-flies with the landing net when a good lake trout has finally got its head up, will not, in my view, be beloved for long.

I always take girlfriends, or possible girlfriends, fishing. For one thing the quietness and the solitude provoke conversation. You can talk about many things and various on the bank of some agreeable pond or mere. And you would be surprised at what comes out. More importantly she can see the hunter-gatherer at work, in all his caveman glory. Or if I catch something she can, anyway. If she tells me "Keep the pressure on, fathead," and gets the net in the water in a meaningful way, I know there is a future in the whole thing. But if she squeals and calls it "Poor

"Keep the pressure on, fathead."

little fishy," then I know that we are heading for the final curtain. If she forearms me out of the way and grabs the rod, muttering "Must I do everything myself?" I venture that there will be lengthy periods of silence during the journey home.

More important still, fishing provides ample opportunity for the grand seduction. I don't suggest vast reservoirs and lonely boats for the purpose. It can be a long row home across a Grafham or a Rutland if the whole things goes awry. But the gentle trickling of water, even if it is down the neck (there is much intimacy to be had under a shared umbrella) and notwithstanding the essential fishiness of the whole operation - what with blood and slime and what-have-you floating about - if during the course of a day, alone and in often glorious surroundings, with a picnic and a decent Chablis, you can't get said what needs to be said, then you are no fisherman, my son.

Having said which, one has to remember that the fatal pheremone works both ways and you may unleash unknown forces. There can be monsters lurking even in the most gentle streams. And still waters run deep and that sort of thing. You would not be the first fisherman to return from the riverbank with no more than a rueful smile and his tackle broken.

She can see the hunter-gatherer at work.

Missing Coco

What do I want for Christmas this year? World peace, goodwill to all and sundry. Not perhaps universal. I will forbear to wish actual ill-will on those nitwits, flower pluckers, tree huggers and bunny cuddlers who persist in meddling in my legitimate pursuits, but I shall go no further. Likewise the spineless politicos who sidle up to such congregations of wasted space and seek to befriend them with their weasel words. For them no goodwill whatever. But for the rest, sweetness and light. And a penny in the poor man's cap.

But what I really want, and the irony here is that this lies in the hands of those same gibbering hordes in Westminster and Whitehall, is to have one more day with my dog.

Recent recruits to the burgeoning pantheon of *Shooting Gazette* readers may not be aware that I have, or have had, a dog. Well, I did. Or sort of did. Coco belonged not to me, but to a dear friend. I was Coco's godfather, mentor, moral guardian and provider of shooting entertainments.

Coco was a labrador; brown in the days when brown was rare; and big. Big on a scale all-too-seldom seen in these days of fast and whippety labs who are more at home in urban flats and small cars, than in the rough waters and open boats of Newfoundland. We forget, most of us, that labradors were designed for waterwork in the rough seas of the North American Atlantic coast. Dragging lines from boat to boat. Hauling distant crab-pot cables to hand; and collaring the occasional sailor who pitched into the surf after one more tot than was strictly required to keep out the hard weather. Coco was built on such historical lines.

When she charged into the brush after game, trees trembled in her wake. When she dived thunderously into lakes and rivers to secure birds, the water did the sensible thing and sought solace elsewhere in tidal waves. When Coco was pleased to see you, that great rudder swept whole occasional tables clear of crockery in a single wiggle of her

Coco

famous, vasty brown bottom. Indeed cups, coffee, a year's collection of the *Shooting Gazette* and often the table itself would be scattered broad-cast about the room as Coco enthused her welcome. Her embarrassment at the ensuing chaos only made matters worse as she stared round in horror at the shambles and sought redemption by rolling on her back and inviting all and sundry to show their forgiveness by tickling her broad tummy.

In addition Coco endeared herself to everyone by her idiosyn-crasy. We all think our dogs are simply the best. Coco was simply different. Coco did not like to be disappointed when in the field. Sitting to attention at my peg, she would watch my performance with a critical eye. When I missed she would exhale a great sigh. If I missed again she would give a snort of derision. After a third fluff she would lie down with her paws over her ears, too ashamed even to be associated with such a duffer. On one memorable occasion she actually walked off, and sat at the feet of one of my neighbours, gazing up enraptured as he slotted pheasant after pheasant for her personal delectation.

Nor did she retrieve as other dogs. Quite apart from her tendency to collect pheasants two at a time, there was none of this "Hi lost!"-ing hither and yon with Coco. I tried it once at a posh shoot and the look she delivered in my direction has me waking up screaming even now. No. At the end of a drive Coco would wait until my gun was in its slip, and then she would set off to retrieve my birds. Not in the order I had shot them; or in the order they were lying. But in the order of neces-sity.

She started with any runners. Dead birds could wait, after all. She had a good nose, but a keener eye, and would have line and distance clearly marked before she set off. Then she would erupt into a gallop, gaining speed and momentum as she went, and many a strong cock, legging its way across the plough towards some distant hedge, has been startled more than somewhat to be body slammed by Coco going at pace. She got me in the knees, once, by mistake, after misjudging a fast turn during a scurry, and the pair of us went base over apex in all directions.

We played in the summer too, at scurries and occasional trials.

She embarrassed me once by collecting the dummy-chucker's bucket, complete with half a dozen dummies, to which she added her own retrieve en route. Practicality was her watchword, and screw the rules. "You want dummies; here's dummies. Get the job done, and Devil take the hindmost. Dummy."

And then she emigrated. Or rather her Mum did. To France. And Coco went too. And there they live now, in the midst of the vineyards of Bordeaux. Lying in the autumn sun, flicking lazily at the butterflies, and stalking an occasional lizard in the grasses beside the pool. It's been five years since they went away, and she's eleven now. She's by no means as big as she was, and she does not bound across the plough as once she did. But the will is still there; and the wiggle. And when occasionally I visit, she rootles through my bag as soon as I put it down, in search of the shooting stockings which will herald a proper day on the morrow. And when she doesn't find them, there are no recriminations. She is still pleased to see me; and we will find something else to do tomorrow to fill the time.

But if I could have one thing for sure this Christmas, all others aside, it would be a passport for Coco. So that she and I could have another day in the frost and the snow and the ice. One more day. Before it's too late.

Goliath

Now there is a fish called Goliath. Or "a Goliath" is, I suppose, the way we should refer to it, it being a species, rather than any old fish. Not least because it is far from being any old fish. Very far indeed. Now it might have been a complete spoof, but I saw it in a book so it must be true.

And if it is a complete spoof, then the fact that I am telling you about it now just shows that because something is not exactly tickety-boo 100 per cent candid shouldn't necessarily get in the way of a good story. As any fisherman in a bar, on the right side of a glass or two of the foaming or the amber or the eau de vie d'Ecosse or whatever knows only too well.

Anyhow this Goliath loiters about in Africa, in the Congo as I recall, or the Zambezi, where it strikes fear and trembling into locals and visitors alike, and is generally more feared and trembled over than the crocodile. The reason being that Goliath is actually piranha's big brother. Now one definition of a dangerous fish is the scale of its teeth. This makes the great white shark really quite a snapper. A great white shark's teeth make up something like three per cent of its body mass. Johnny Piranha on the other hand is about 30 per cent teeth. Which makes him a very scary fish indeed. But piranha is a small fish. Perhaps as big as your hand. The scary bit is that they go around in gangs. The reason the water boils and the unfortunate animal or secret agent or whatever looks so uncomfortable is because there are a zillion of the little brutes all having a simultaneous nibble.

Goliath, au contraire, is a very big fish indeed. Tens of kilos springs to mind. And a third of that is teeth. So you don't need very many nibbles on that scale before severe discomfort is experienced. Hence the fear and trembling.

Your crocodile lurks about the corner of the pond or river and waits until some gormless individual, human or wildebeest, sticks some part of himself in the water. Then crocodile, as the Elephant's child tells us, takes a good firm grip and hoicks said gormless into the drink. After which, as a matter of fact, he drags his prey to the bottom and lies on it until it goes quiet.

Goliath does nothing of the sort. Goliath cruises about the place – maybe here, maybe there – until he sees something or someone in the water; and then he shoots in at top speed and bites off a chunk and away. Meanwhile the unfortunate victim wades ashore in a startled condition to take a look at what's missing. Or rather to take a look at the place where what is now missing used to be. Now you don't need telling what the soft targets are, do you? So there's a thought to shrink the tackle.

Expert fishermen, for whom the Goliath is a fish at the top end of the sporting hit parade, pursue him with spinning rods and flashing lures attached by piano wire traces. And we are not talking about the high notes either. And this is done from the back of a narrow dug-out canoe which is notoriously wobbly at the best of times and certainly no less wobbly when it has a 40 kilo Goliath attached to it by a wire trace, fifty yards of strong monofilament and two yards of over-excited sportsman. And apparently the key point of debate among those sporting types who thus pursue the Goliath is at what point does the excitement reach a crescendo? Is it the moment of strike when the mighty fish hits the lure? Or is it during the titanic battle that inevitably follows? Or is it at that moment of high drama when some idiot actually hauls the damn fish over the gunwale and suddenly sundry sportspersons, guides, paddlers and so forth find themselves joined by what may be described as a seventy five pound turbocharged pike with attitude. On speed.

I was reminded of this the other day when I was boating on the pond in the park. The very glamorous remote control model 14 Ms were back in the clubhouse having battled through a miniature Americas Cup. The speed boats had all run out of lighter fuel. It was my turn. I wound up my tug to its fullest extent and set it off across the water. As tugs will it proceeded at a stately pace to the middle of the pond, where it stopped and bobbed. It's a round pond and not very big and there was a breeze rippling the surface and I had nothing on my hands but time. If I waited long enough my tug would gradually bob back to me.

However one of two youths who had watched, not without

mirth at my expense I may say, nonetheless offered to wade out and fetch it. "I'll gerrit forra fiver, mate," he said. So I thought about it and offered him a quid and holding his shorts high, for all the water came just above his knees, he set off gingerly in pursuit.

And while he went, I related to his companion the story of Goliath. And he paled somewhat and asked where such a fish was to be found, and I said I thought still, shallow water where people waded and he went a bit paler and then he shouted "Oi! Ma-ate!! Bloke 'ere says there's a fish in 'ere'll 'ave yer knackers orf! Gerrart, mate!! Gerrart!" Whereupon 'is mate began floundering and stumbling back to the side where he arrived in due season shaken and soaking. Much to my secret satisfaction.

Which goes to show that it really does not matter whether it is a spoof or not as long as your audience believes you. As any fisherman knows.

I said in August, I would shoot a grouse this year.

Grousing Revisited

I said in August I would shoot a grouse this year and I did. And it was as completely satisfactory as I had expected it to be. No surprises so far. There's no going back though, is there? "The follies of men's youth are in retrospect glorious compared to the follies of their old age." I don't know who said it, but he was bang on the money in my view and he knew a deal about what it is to be a chap to boot.

We mustered at the weekend in a commodious lodge in what can only be described as Scotland. It was somewhere near Inverness, that's for sure, but quite where I really couldn't tell you. And I'm not just being coy because of the cost of libel suits these days: I'm not telling you because one bit of Scotland looks very much like another to me. Soaring majestic crags lower over dappled slopes above purplish abundances of heather. It's just lovely and as poetic as you could wish for and there's another great swathe of it next door in the neighbouring glen so that working out quite which glen exactly you are in is something of a secondary issue when all is said and done. I did try to look it up on the Ordnance Survey map that someone left lying about the place but I could not make head nor tail of the damn thing and I'm far from certain that I had it the right way up at the time anyway. I think we might have been between the church with a steeple and the big hill, or that might have been the ring from someone's coffee cup. Orienteering was never my strong point.

Anyway it was all rendered academic because we had Angus, our genial host, to do our thinking for us. And Angus had clearly been doing enough thinking not only for us but for a small army. Which, Angus, being an ex-soldier – sorry, ex-cavalry officer – is clearly the sort of body of folk Angus is comfortable thinking for.

So before the grouse outing, before even sitting down actually and getting my tonsils round something of a gargle after the thick end of twelve hours on a variety of trains with all the horrors that implies, we were getting into a host of briefings about what we were going to get up to for the week. Sit. Rep. Chaps all here. Disposition of troops.

…with legs going like pistons.

You're in this room, they're in that room. Cook's in there. Dogs there or thereabouts. Wife and veg somewhere else. Lights out stop talking. Rations – adequate until about Wednesday, after that we have to shoot something, catch something else or mount a raiding party on Tesco's. Whisky – abundant. Ammunition – plentiful. Weather outlook – fine with scattered showers; depression over Ireland; mounting pressure in the kitchen already since someone forgot the sausages. Breakfast at 0800, small arms drill at 0930 followed by training march up to the loch and back for lunch. You can take the man out of the army, but.......

We got to the moor on Wednesday, since you ask, and a very agreeable sort of a grousing day it promised to be. An early highlight was the sight of the commander-in-chief himself legging it straight back down the steep and windy track, tweedy gaiter-shod legs going like the proverbial clappers, in pursuit of his good lady wife, who was going kindly to fetch sundry kids and, crucially, lunch for a rendezvous later when he realised that he had neglected to collect his gun, cartridges and dogs from the car before sending her on her way with a kiss and a cheery wave. I couldn't swear that she was letting him catch up a little before accelerating round the next corner each time, but then I couldn't swear that she wasn't either.

We had time though for a fag and a breather though before the C-in-C, blowing a bit, was back to make his dispositions. We lined out in the heather. The sun shone. Grouse called. We started walking. And, speaking entirely personally now you understand, encountered the combined effects of a decade of modestly riotous living, a spot of claret here and there and a deal of steam pudding almost immediately. I suppose the slope is a necessary feature of hills, but do they have to be quite that steep? And why always up? And up? And up?

The keeper was loping along through the heather and it was not very long before our tidy line looked rather more like the retreat of the 44th from Gandamack, with bodies lying here and there in the brush, children wailing and grown men putting on a brave face in front of the girls.

There is iron though in the soul of the Boys' Team (of myth and legend). The flesh may be weak and significantly more abundant than once it was, but the spirit is the spirit of grousehunters for all that. And so we marched, and as we marched, sundry grouse put up pockets of token resistance here and there about the moor and were duly bagged. We made the peak by early afternoon and the rendezvous with more spouses and offspring and, critically, lunch with grouse and with honour.

"We'll just pause for a moment," said Angus, "and then I'll brief you on how we are going to manage the afternoon." On the hill, sun on your face, grouse in the bag.

I admit I may have dozed a while.

Happy Families

I've bought a sea-fishing rod. And before you all start getting aerated and writing in that Catchpole's taking the whole thing to new and unacceptable lows and chaps don't fish at sea unless marooned on desert islands or cast away in lifeboats from their yachts by unruly staff, just let me tell you why.

This being summer I have been sitting on the beach a good deal and sitting on the beach one day I saw a chap fishing. Way down the sand he was, on a spit that ran out along the estuary. Casting into the tide. Back and forth until the gathering tide drove him back along the strand towards the harbour. Once the tide was full, he threw his rod into a smartly varnished crab-boat of the sort we have in these parts – 12 foot stem to stern, $1^1/_2$ horsepower diesel, draw about a foot – and off he chugged home, I guessed. But even as the tide ebbed he was back; casting once again into the receding water and making steady progress back up the spit.

I watched him for a couple of days. He didn't look local. Though what is local in a village that has a winter population of 400, mostly retired solicitors and investment bankers, and a summer population of ten times that though still largely made up of lawyers and bankers and their wives and children and their childrens' friends and their Mercedes and their dogs and au pairs and boats and buckets and spades and all the paraphernalia of the English at home but away? At the same time though he didn't look like a visitor either, what with the crab-boat and the way he came and went with the tides without getting stranded which is what the visitors tend to do.

I saw one the other day on the quay absolutely beside himself with fury and remonstrating with the boatman because the water wasn't where it was supposed to be. He'd been down first thing and there was water everywhere but now he'd been to fetch his boat it had drained away just as if the plug had been pulled and who the hell had the right to go about the place doing things like that, he would like to know? The

boatman was trying to explain the concept of tides to him, but by the time he'd got onto the relative gravitational pulls of varying states of the lunar cycle the bloke had stormed off in a huff and was taking it out on his trailer tyres. But there you go.

This chap didn't look like one of those. So on the third day I waited until the water had driven him back along the sand and he was reeling in with that air of finality which indicates a last cast and I accosted him in the traditional manner. "Any luck?" says I. "None," says he. "What are you after?" says I. "I'm not sure, to be honest," he says. "I suppose you might find a bass out there, or perhaps whiting. Mackerel, for sure, from time to time and there is always a chance, I suppose, that you might with luck get into a sea-trout if you happened to have an evening tide just about spot on." "What are you using?" I asked. He thrust the handle of the rod towards me and there was a simple brass spoon hooked into the bottom of the reel. "Mark you," he says "catching things is not actually the point."

Well, at that moment, of course, I knew that local or not he was a fellow fisherman. "For sure," says I, "but then again, a fish now and again is better than nothing. Recharges the batteries of hope and stiffens the sinews and all that?" "Actually no," he replied. "I really mean that catching things is not the point."

Then why, I enquired, was he fishing? And fishing diligently for that matter? Tide after tide? Day after day?

He looked at me with a wistful smile. "I have a house here, holiday home, had it a lot of years actually. We always come here in the summer. When the children were small it was next to perfect. Buckets and spades on the beach; swims in the breakers. That sort of thing. But they grow up, you know."

"So now they're all gone and you have taken up fishing?" I ventured.

"Christ, no!" says he "I've got four daughters at home ranging from fifteen down to seven. The older ones have boyfriends who communicate only in grunts and the younger ones have girlfriends who speak only in shrieks and giggles. My parents-in-law are staying for a week and then my parents are coming. My wife has two spaniels. My mother," he took a deep breath, "is bringing her cat."

"It must," I said, "be quite a big house." He looked at me for a long moment before answering. "I can see you are not a family man," he said. I nodded. "It is a very large house. The point, however, is that," and here his voice trembled slightly, "it is not big enough. So I bought a fishing rod."

With which he cranked the rotor of his $1^1/_2$ horsepower diesel and chugged off down the tideway.

When I got home the light was blinking on the answering machine. The first message started "Since the weather looks set for this weekend we were wondering......?" The second began "Are you all alone down there because the kids asked me to ask you, since the weather looks.......?" I am not a family man. The third message was from my mother.

I have bought a sea fishing rod.

When the children were small, it was next to perfect...

The grey ghost of the birdtable.

Nutkin

"I really wish they wouldn't do that!" Do what? says I. "Steal the food off the bird table," she says. And that, as they say, is when the out-of-season sportsman really perks up his ears and begins to take a bit of notice. Children bashing ten kinds of hell out of one another? All part of growing up. Dogs digging holes in lawns? Don't bribe the poor dears with bones then.

But someone, something, nicking food off bird tables implies pesky varmints and pesky varmints always offer a sporting opportunity if handled properly. If it's the cats again then we may have to be a bit restrained. The cat issue had already got me into tepid water a few years ago, but even so a Supa-Soaker 600 pump action water pistol can still offer a diverting and non-terminal morning's entertainment.

I sought further and better particulars. "Who or what is stealing food off the bird table?" "Squirrels," she says. "Can't you do something about it?" Could I ever?

The point is that these opportunities come only from time to time. The bunnies marauding about the garden are Flopsy, Mopsy and Cottontail until they get in among the borders and do an Agent Orange on the perennials. Reynard is a Foxy-Woxy until he gets at the chickens. Even the blasted magpies are headwaiters until they are caught *in flagrante* with a thrush egg in their beaks. Squirrels are all bushy tailed Nutkins until a moment like this when they are demoted, quite summarily and cursorily I notice, to the tree rats they truly are.

Still that's women for you. Mother Teresa one minute, Cruella de Ville the next. Don't you just love them?

Still, the opportunity was not to be missed. I equipped myself with an air rifle in the first instance. A .22, mark you, with a telescope on top and a decent spring within - no fairground fart gun this – and parked myself in the garden shed with a tin of pellets and the crossword to ambush the next grey ghost of the bird table.

I didn't have to wait terribly long. "Girl likely to make a big impression (4,4)" adequately summarises the result. Wide miss, since you ask. He was certainly a somewhat startled Nutkin as the pellet whanged comprehensively into the woodwork beside him, but deterred he was not.

Now a bad workman blames his tools and I am content to join the union for the time being. There are mornings when I would certainly own up to being an easy half-foot off the mark accuracy-wise but this was not one of them. Obviously the zero was squiffy. So I went and got a beer can and having emptied it in the traditional fashion, I took it down the garden and gave it a serious pasting for a few minutes until I was content that, trembling hands notwithstanding, the 'scope was up to the mark'. Then I returned to my ambush in the potting shed. In the meantime Nutkin had cleared out the rest of the resources on the bird table and pushed off. He didn't come back either. Even when I had loaded the thing down with crisps and peanuts.

If the mountain won't come to Mahomet…. So I went looking for the mountain. But before I did, I exchanged the air rifle for one of the 16 bores, because while an air rifle is a good tool for garden stalking and a 16 bore really isn't; in woodland the scatter-gun comes into its own.

He wasn't hard to find. Follow the line of dead and dying trees with the bark neatly stripped. It's shocking, really, the damage they do when you start looking at it with forester's eyes – or tree owner's anyway – instead of rose-tinted B. Potter specs.

I caught up with him among the beeches and there followed a brief and vigorous pursuit as he dashed up one trunk, along a branch or three and down the next with yours truly pounding along behind trying to get something approaching a clear shot. I did get one barrel off but the effect was no more than a face full of twigs. And then I ran into a tree.

"Take a view for a full house (4,4)" would seem to fit the bill. Bingo! Eyes down. And a moment later so was I. The squirrel sat up the tree and laughed. At least I imagine he did, but I wasn't seeing too well at this juncture because of the stars.

So I had tried the rapier and I had tried the sledgehammer. I had tried stealth and I had tried hot pursuit. None had worked. It was clearly time to cheat.

Twilight therefore found me back in the beeches with the .22 rimfire, several beers and the crossword. I sat for an hour with my back against a trunk and the rifle across my knees, a tinny within reach and struggled with 24 Across "Latecomer makes it just in time (4,2,7)" I looked up under the hat brim now and again and sure enough there he was. Sitting on a bough eating a freshly filched bird-table crisp. Slowly, slowly catchee Nutkin. A click, a phhutt and down he came. And with him came 24 Across. "Dead on arrival."

I went back to the house and left him on the kitchen table while I returned the rifle to the cabinet. As I turned the key I heard a shriek from downstairs. "I really wish you wouldn't do that!" she said.

Like I said – don't you just love them?

Misconduct

I don't know whether I should tell you this. But it's been on my conscience for a long time and I think I might feel better if I get it off my chest. I did once cheat. A bit. Well, actually I'm not altogether sure that I did. I didn't know that there were rules in the first place, so it was not as if I meant to ignore them. I just didn't know. I realise that *ignorans non excusatus* is a principle of English law, but maybe if I set the record straight I can get the whole thing knocked back to troutslaughter on appeal. It's not as if I lobbed a grenade into the Spey after all.

Anyway there was a gillie with me and he never so much as blinked. Mark you he may have been a frightfully good gillie who took the view that it is not the proper place of a good gillie to criticise a fishing gentleman on the riverside, however crass his behaviour.

Or perhaps he was a bad gillie who was merely expecting me to slip him a bribe commensurate with the crime. Either way he was in for a big disappointment.

Are they gillies in Hampshire, by the way, or is that an exclusively Scots term? Or are they ghillies anyway? The more I write it the stranger it looks. I'm never sure; and certainly too in awe of them ever to ask. Perhaps they are water-bailiffs, or riverkeepers in the soft south. Guides in Ireland. To hell with it, there was a professional fisher-bloke with me at the time and he never said nowt.

This was the way of it.

I was bidden, in my capacity as journo and great all-round expert in things sporting, to a newly formed sporting paradise in Hampshire. I forget where exactly, it might have been Berkshire now I come to think of it. Still the where is not important. The object of the exercise was for me, and others like me, to experience and assess the delights of the place in order that we would give the outfit the benefit of our gushing praise in print, which would save them the tedious necessity of having to advertise their wares to the wealthy sportsmen whom they wished to part from a goodly wedge of ackers for the privilege of becoming members.

There was to be shooting and fishing and golf and archery and hawking and four wheel driving and all manner of wonderful opportunities on display for our delectation. And doubtless there would be refreshments in abundance to boot. And at the very heart of the operation was a decent stretch of one of our justly famous chalkstreams; neatly trimmed, clear as gin, and manifestly populated by brown trout on a significant scale. It was, in short, exactly the sort of glorious jolly that you lot think we lot get all the time, but which actually comes along once in a blue moon. Or more particularly which falls off the magazine Editor's desk once in a blue moon. But that's another matter.

The trouble was that I had been on an equally glorious toot the previous night. On my own wallet, I might add, and was, on the morning in question as the policeman's notebook says, paying for it big time. I was, to put it bluntly, monstrously hungover and generally feeling extremely sorry for myself. In which condition the ideas variously of shooting or golfing, or as it might be hawking or four wheel driving, or indeed talking, moving or even breathing real fast were enough to elicit a soft moan and no more. Fishing on the other hand, I felt I could manage. Standing garden gnome style, beside the tranquil stream, in a soft and balmy breeze, would do me handsome until lunch-time at the earliest. Accordingly I shambled along to the fishing hut and was issued with a rod and accompanied by the whatchemacallit bloke took myself off to find a convenient spot to cast in, or throw up, whichever happened first.

I found a sort of backwater out of the way and duly cast. I flipped the little rod back and forth a few times and duly caught the tree immediately behind me. "Bugger!" says I, not loud. I tugged the fly free, flipped some more and plonked the thing directly into the reeds on the other side of the stream. "Bugger!" says I, though still not loud. And there I'm bound to record the thing stayed. I got the leader back alright, but of flies, baits and lures, there was no sign whatever. "Oi!" says I to the water bloke, "Have you a fly about you? I've lost this one." He didn't. Or perhaps he did, but didn't trust me with it; which is understandable.

Well, hungover and generally disinterested I may have been, but I draw the line at fishing without a fly. So I removed my hat, and detached from it the remains of some elderly imitation with which the thing is decorated, or more exactly held together. I don't know what it was, even when it was something; but it was a very sorry looking something now. It looked more or less as I felt. Nonetheless, I tied him on and bunged him in, and he sank. And that's my sin, you see. That's the rule on these chic-est of chic chalkstreams. Dry-fly only and always cast up-stream. Not whatever falls out of the box and heave it where you will. Anyway I didn't know and I cared even less.

The trout, *au contraire*, had not seen anything this exciting in months. None of your namby-pamby imitations delicately landed gossamer-like on the surface just above your glistening brown nose. Any self respecting chalkstream trout knows what that means. Here though was a great black woolly thing sploshing heartily and heavily about the place. Clearly elevenses had arrived. And Christmas. The fly, such as it was, was duly galumphed by the biggest fish in the vicinity which elbowed, or perhaps finned, his way to the front of the maul and swallowed the offending article in one gulp.

I will not weary you with the details of the effect this strike had on me upstairs, except to say that if you take a good friend by the shoulders when he is nursing something similar, and rattle him back and forth for several minutes, any further explanation will be redundant. I was not, I'm afraid, a sympathetic or sporting or appreciative fisherman that morning. I played him only cursorily and then dragged the brute onto the bank and told the water-wallah to deal with things while I had a personal moment or two.

And the final irony - they gave me a prize. The damn thing was record for the stretch. I got a magnum of champagne. I couldn't have taken it for all the tea in China. Partially through guilt, but mostly because the sight of it made me ill again. I gave it to the gillie person who took it, kept a straight look, a straight face and his counsel.

That's my confession. The matter is now a matter for you. Your judgement, the judgement of a body empanelled from my peers, is now all that remains to be determined. Pish! Enough of this nonsense. Confession is a thirsty business. Whose round is it?

... a gentleman should always wear a hat.

Hormones

This being Spring, my hormones are on the rampage. After a long and mercifully dormant winter, the first touch of watery sun on the old bonce sends testosterone charging round the system like a mad thing, a faraway look resides in the eyes and the lip lolls. It's sad but true.

That is why nanny said that a gentleman should be careful always to wear a hat.

Shakespeare suggested that there are seven ages of man and so there may be, but frankly I think he was talking through the very hat that his nanny probably insisted upon. It has taken some working out but I reckon that I have the theory pretty much formulated now.

There are four seasons; and they go like this. In the winter I hibernate. I emerge from time to time to participate in things like Christmas, but basically I am out of commission during the coldest part of the year. Autumn is harvest time. A great deal of pursuit is undertaken, collecting fish and fowl and whatever with rods and guns to provide the wherewithal to get through the dark months ahead. During the summer I work. While others are basking on sundrenched beaches and getting stuck into bad novels the size of doorstops and smearing themselves and others with unguents and balms, I am beavering away doing whatever has to be done to make sure that the rest of the year is more or less free for hunting expeditions; and in the Spring, well, in the Spring I find myself seething with hormones and undertaking pursuits of a very different kind. There is more pursuing than any other part of the proceedings, indeed it is mostly pursuing, but life was ever thus.

Now I dare say that there will be those who will be inclined to pooh-pooh these thoughts, but think it through and I wager you will see more than a shred of truth in the whole thing. Man is an animal after all, and not so far removed from the primal as all that. And those of us who are inclined to fish are probably less far removed than most. The old instincts are closer to the surface than we would perhaps like to believe.

For a start the wardrobe changes. The dull and muted shades of winter, the heavy and sensible tweeds are consigned once more to the back of the cupboard and the brighter, sprucer and lighter garb is once more to the fore. We summon up the nerve to visit our tailor, or even to brave the sales in the high street. This is no more than mating plumage. Birds, bears, and for all I know bees, shed the thick and shaggy drabness of winter and re-emerge vibrant and sleek for the amorous challenges ahead. What else is spring cleaning but a mucking out of the winter quarters preparatory to luring the quarry of the moment into the privacy of the scented boudoir without her throwing up her hands in horror and inadvertently disturbing the dust of ages?

A pal of mine went further. He used to redecorate his apartment every Spring without fail. Builders and decorators would move in for weeks, year after year, while he went about seeking whom he might devour. The tradesmen and artisans were generally thrown out again before the final coat of paint was applied, or the last kitchen appliance fitted. He said it saved time next year and money this. He said there was nothing so attractive to women than being asked their opinion about the new curtains. And he was right. Up to point. The problem was that

he was always chasing and luring the most colourful potential mates and they were less concerned with chintz than perhaps they should have been. He was a sucker for a bit of plumage. Six inch heels, a micro-mini and a spandex boob tube and he was away to the races and no mistake. Into the two seater, roof down and back to the newly refurbished love-nest was the idea. The difficulty arose later when the madness of Spring subsided.

During the summer he worked like a demon, toiling diligently at the coal-face, as you do, and filling evenings and weekends with trysts and passion. But it is hard work burning the candle at both ends like this, and gradually as early urges waned and the heavy tweeds and sensible boots began once more to emerge from the wardrobe as summer's lease was ended, the bright and spangly companions would drift off in pursuit of more electrifying company. And he would get down to the more serious business of tying his flies for the grilse runs, greasing his reels, polishing his ferrules and checking his diary for available dates for the forthcoming seasonal highlights.

Until, that is, he met the one who recognised the cycle. It is true that the whole thing began in the Spring, as these things will; but as the summer wore on she didn't drift off. While he toiled, she actually finished the redecoration of the house. She chose the curtains and fitted the carpets, and re-arranged the furniture. She went with him to river-banks and lakesides and she cheered him as he netted fish; and stayed discreetly silent when he did not. She went with him to the hills and woods and forests and applauded as he collected stags and pheasants and carried them home in triumph. That winter they hibernated. The rest is history. The following Spring the builders and decorators were dismissed when they called for their annual contracts. The furniture remained where it was. The wedding soon followed.

All of which tells us what we already knew. That even though the water is heaving with fish and notwithstanding the right lure, the right conditions, the right place and a following wind, a delicacy of touch in the cast which would do credit to a brain surgeon, success is still a question of fine timing because it's all for naught if the quarry's not in the mood. It's a lurve thang.

Last Week

There are few things in this life that can be relied upon. Apart, of course, from death and taxes. With the end of the tax year coming up both are weighing somewhat heavily upon the mind. You're born, you work, you pay taxes, you die. QED. RIP. Bit of a bleak outlook, isn't it? Another thing that can be relied upon is that you can't trust the government. We should remember this very carefully. Especially with this government. They are out to get us. They have hunting in their sights right now and although they say that they have no intention of interfering with fishing, they also told us the Dome was a good idea and would be sold for millions afterwards and that Railtrack shareholders wouldn't get a bean. Ha! How many of the Cabinet fish? They don't fish! Not with a fly, nor a worm, nor with a 'umble humble. So they don't care one way or the other.

I know that lots of folk fish but we are still a minority and we are neither metropolitan nor vocal. And that puts us at risk. You saw the PETA ads. Those misguided airheads have $30 million in their back pockets from deluded, guilt-stricken bunny huggers around the world and a million bucks buys an awful lot of policy from the folk in Westminster these days. Fishing is a gentle pastime which does no harm to anyone; but not everyone can do it. It ain't free for all at the point of delivery. It's exclusive. You need an invitation. Or money. Or both. So just you mind your backs and when the word comes to descend on Westminster to ram the point home, you get out there and descend and ram with the rest. If you think it can't happen to you, take a look at the collective madness that has infected Scotland. They haven't banned fishing yet, but they are going to confiscate it in the meantime.

Enough. For the time being.

I just got a postcard from Tierra del Fuego, from a nice old boy I met recently. He's made a bit and now spends his time floating round the world visiting friends and places and doing a spot of fishing betimes. He's done it all. Big fish, sail fish, bonefish, tigerfish, permit, tarpon, shark – you name it, he's had a lash at it. He's been everywhere. Well, almost

everywhere, and anywhere he hasn't been is on the list to be visited in due course. He's fished the US and Canada; England and Scotland, Eire, Scandiland, Russia, Iceland, Oz and New Zealand. He's pretty much fished the globe. The postcard said "Guide reports we should have been here last week!"

It's a truth universally recognised. The answer, of course, is not to visit, but to live beside your fishing. I freely admit to being jealous of those who can fish at the foot of the garden. It makes no odds whether home is a great granite castle beside a surging torrent in the Highlands – or as it might be a croft beside a surging torrent in the Highlands, for that matter – or a Chilean estancia or a log cabin in Kiwi land or a commuter box in Berkshire, if it has a bit of water through it; that's luxury. Any time of the night or day, as the mood takes you, you can slip out of the door with a rod and a lure and potter down to the water's edge for a dangle. But far and away the best aspect is that when you live beside your water there is no "last week" any more. The gillie, bailiff, keeper, guide, professional – whoever – can't say "….you should have been here last week," because you were. And the week before. And next week too. You've got him cold. Every single day.

There is a bit of a drawback though. Which is that you can never leave. Because the moment you leave, you have to come back and that vital leverage is gone. That's why my friend is fishing in Tierra del Fuego. He's a rich bloke and a keen angler; you'd think he'd have a bit of water to call his own and you'd be right. And he had a bloke who managed it for him. Not a great red bearded gillie to be sure, but a professional for all that. And he was content because he could never be told what he had missed last week. But he left it for a spell and, of course, now he can never go back. So he's become a sort of piscatorial Flying Dutchman, cruising round the world, putting in here and there to fish. And always being a week late.

He's been everywhere.

Open Season

There's been a bit of a conflab down at the pond. It's been known to happen from time to time, but generally speaking, nothing can be relied upon to happen. It's known, rather grandly, as the AGM but tends to more usually take the form of a post-season party where the syndicate picks up the tab for the beer. Pretty sound, you might say.

One pitches along, if inclined, one hoovers up a tincture or three and as many peanuts as the pockets will handle, one mingles a bit, exaggerating wildly betimes about the size and ferocity of the fish one has caught or more probably lost over the years – or depending on the tincture consumption and the gender and demeanour of one's interlocutor – the size and ferocity of other things, such as prostates or bunions or wives or dogs or panic attacks or tax demands or whatever springs to mind really - and finally one beams hither and yon and takes oneself off.

Only this year it was different. There was, apparently, an agenda.

I didn't notice it myself, I must say; but then I am, by my own admission, a creature of habit and I might have been concentrating somewhat on the tinctures and peanuts department rather than focussing on the conversation.

At least during the early part of the evening. Later, of course, I would have been focussing a great deal more on the conversation, given that by then it takes all my concentration to remember what I am talking about or to whom. Or where they are. Or where I am. Or why.

However, this year, and I do mean this year now, the other day, I got Minutes. Whole bunch of them. Great long list. Pages. It must have been quite a lively discussion, I shouldn't wonder. I don't recall it myself, really, but I might have popped out for a bit of fresh air perhaps, or something.

Anyway the upshot is that we have, according to the Minutes, so it must be true, abolished the holidays. It's right there in black and white. Henceforth we are fishing year round. Apparently you can do this now. Though since when I couldn't say. So there you have it. No more closed season. Get those rods out right now and look sharp about it.

Now, I'm not wholly against this, I must say. It's just that it's a bit of a departure. I mean, we would be starting the season right about now anyway, as I recall, so there is not much of a difference there anyway. Where there will be a difference will be the other end of the season. On the upside, of course, there will be the advantage of arriving at the pond and being able to fish, instead of what usually happens which is that I pole up mid October and find a big notice on the gate saying "Closed". (It's October, Stupid! DUH!") and have to go home again.

On the other hand, there is the issue of biking up to the pond in the deep midwinter. This requires a deal more gear than a summer run. In the dog days, it is a matter of simply strapping on rods and nets and zooming off and away. If anything, in the summer months, it is keeping cool under the leathers which is the problem, and early runs out and late returns are all the thing.

Winter is quite a different set of thermals altogether. I once did a journey – more by accident than design, it must be said, I'd started, as it were, so I had to finish – in freezing fog. Not only was it terrifying beyond belief, but my vizor kept icing up on the inside and when I opened it, my lips and eyeballs froze. I kid you not. I made it home; but I did spend the rest of the day in the bath trying to thaw myself.

Quite apart from which, I shall doubtless need a whole bunch of winter tackle. What do trout eat in the winter? Exactly? I shall need books; and flies. Lines, I shouldn't wonder. And reels. This may entail a whole new approach. This is serious. And seriously expensive.

I can understand, mark you, why we've done it. Given that the average age of the team is about a million and two, anything which maximises the time spent fishing is a given. When you reach this sort of age, time becomes a commodity more precious than jewels of great price and harder to get hold of, and time spent fishing is the most precious of the lot.

I don't recall voting for it, but on the whole I don't mind. I think. I'll treat it as a normal season and find out how it feels at the end, when we just carry on. It will be a little strange, I suspect, for a while but I'm not too old to change. I wonder what else we decided.

Ground Defence

My heart always sinks a little when I hear the words "No ground game, please." Or perhaps I should say, since it is hard for my heart to sink at all on a shooting morning, that my spirits rise a little when I hear: "By all means shoot ground game, where you can."

There was a time, not really so long ago, when I was a beater for the most part, but also in my early days as a Gun, when ground game, hares particularly and rabbits, used to make up a significant proportion of the bag on any shooting day. A glance through the older Game Books shows that on a modest day of a hundred or so head of game, there would be perhaps twenty hares and a handful of rabbits.

I miss the ground game. I know that in many parts of the country hares are now comparatively rare, where once they used to flourish; but rabbits are back in a big way these days and yet still seldom figure in any kind of formal shooting.

The principal answer lies in the safety aspect. Now that so many estates let days to strangers, and strangers may bring guests who are stranger still, there is no point in encouraging them to shoot at each others ankles. The birds may not be much to write home about height-wise, but at least when airborne they can usually be relied upon to gain sufficient altitude so that the Guns are shooting upwards and therefore less likely to put beaters, keepers, hosts or each other in the gamecart. This is all to the good and completely understandable, but a Gun who has never shot ground game cannot be said to be, in my view, an experienced Gun.

I was in Norfolk recently, shooting with friends. They are doing sterling work on their farm planting copses and woods and renewing hedges on a portion of the estate that has come back into their hands. They are however plagued by hares and rabbits. They address the rabbit question at all times and in all ways, ferreting, shooting, gassing and netting. The hares they can only really get to grips with on shoot days. They have a formal hare shoot every other year, and bags have, contrary

I saw the shot splatter into the earth.

to expectation, been going consistently up over the last decade, without any discernable improvement in the accuracy of the Guns. Granted, some of the younger Guns (and the hare shoots were mainly for the benefit of younger Guns) may have got older, possibly wiser and conceivably more accurate; but by the same token the older Shots are now increasingly decrepit, mostly ga-ga and hopelessly wide of the mark; so the hares must be on the increase when all is said and done. Your hare is a nibbler, and all about the place is evidence of their passing. A sprig here, a topped planting there; and hares leaping up from beneath the feet left, right and centre as we blank in the broad plough that surrounds each copse or marl pit that form the central objective of each drive.

The wise do not shoot hares early in the operation. Anyone who has carried two or three hares for any distance over heavy ground will tell you that what seemed an enticing shot half a mile or so ago, becomes a worse and worse idea as each furrow becomes a positive Everest and the peg seems to move further away with each mud-laden step. Once on the peg however, the experienced Shots do not hold back and any hare or rabbit ill-advised enough to make a late break for the border is likely to find its exit abruptly and terminally interrupted.

There is though, a real discipline that must be exerted when addressing ground game, that is best gained through experience. With beaters in front, pickers-up behind and fellow Guns either side, the safe area for the despatch of the odd hare is limited and clearly defined. A hare that lollops towards the line is likely to put in a spurt as it passes the Guns and its passage through that vital few yards is often at top speed. It's a one-shot operation, which should not be lightly undertaken and which must be right first time. A wounded hare is a noisy and disturbing sight, but the chance of a second shot is slim. Properly done, a bird in the air and a hare on the ground is a right and left that lingers in the memory. Muffed, it will have you sitting bolt upright in the deep of the night with sheets clenched in sweaty palms and a strangled whimper on the lips.

I saw the perfect example out in the Fens. We were shooting fast Fen pheasants out of miniscule patches of cabbages and kale set amid vast tracts of black plough. There were hares everywhere too. I was in the line next to a farmer friend whose stalwart efforts to reduce agricultural surpluses by shooting four days a week throughout the season seem to have gone largely unnoticed, but who shoots extremely well as a result. He was next to a frightfully smart City broker, whose glossy bespoke everything was harshly at odds with his inability to hit anything at all. In this environment it is crucial to take your pheasants good and early in front and bowl over your hares smartly behind. This point was lost on our Threadneedle street tyro, who consistently attempted to assassinate his hares before and his pheasants aft, with complete lack of success in either direction. When we finally arrived at our respective pegs he had a determined look that prompted me to position myself firmly with poor Roger between us, and hope that no hares came forward.

They did, of course. He had a crack at the first one almost at the beaters' toes, and then followed it carefully round as it romped past Roger's peg. The hare was well behind Roger when our financial friend loosed his second barrel; but since he was well behind the hare I saw the shot splatter into the earth about Roger's boots. Roger did not look a happy farmer at all as he killed the hare well back. He tried to shoo the second hare away, but without success and another brace of cartridges bracketed his peg as our brave Broker sought vainly to get off the mark. Roger, looking grim, bowled it over with his choke barrel. The third one broke the dam. As the shot once again rattled about his leggings and pinged off his shooting stick, Roger took a fine bird over his head, then spun round and shot the hare stone dead behind him.

He then marched out to where the three hares lay almost together and taking them to his neighbour's peg he hurled them at the financier's finely shod feet. There followed from a range of a few inches and in a voice that could have been heard across the Wash a splendid monologue of Fenland vernacular covering all aspects of the merchant's appearance, performance and parentage. "...and if you shoot me again," Roger concluded, "I'll jolly well shoot you back, and I'm a much better shot than you are, so you'll dashed well know it's happened." Loosely translated that's what he said anyway.

As he stomped back to his peg I could see that he was grinning

124

hugely and clearly feeling well pleased, and probably much relaxed, if I'm any judge.

At the end of the drive I ambled across to where Roger was slipping his gun into its sleeve and offered my sympathy. But why had he waited so long to put the sinner to rights? His expression was pure devilment. "I like shooting hares," he said "but I do hate to carry them." He pointed to where the financier was staggering off across the plough, the three hares bumping along beside him. The transport was a distant dot on the horizon. "I reckon by the time yon smartboy has those three in the gamecart for me he'll be a wiser man and a better Shot."

Credit where credit's due, he duly lugged them the whole way, and he did shoot more wisely, if no better, for the rest of the day. Wisdom and experience. Can't be beat.

Do we fish to catch fish?

Less is More

Russia is the new paradise. One week, a handful of rods, 1,000 salmon. Welcome to heaven. You don't even have to die to get there. Not any more. Time was when the journey was more of an adventure than the fishing. Planes, trains and wonky old helicopters which had been resurrected after the Afghan war; or more probably sneaked out of the repair shed while no one was looking. Without being repaired first.

The lodge was a tent in the middle of nowhere. Meals were a mess of potage and some bread. The plumbing made a dunny down the garden path look like the Waldorf Astoria. Now it's five stars all the way. Unremitting luxury. And a thousand salmon in a week. Am I jealous? You bet your cutes, I'm jealous. My score stands, as you well know, at one. And that took several decades to catch; and would have taken several more months to describe adequately, in my view, but the Editor of *Trout and Salmon* decided we must move on, so here we are. Pondering. A thousand salmon in a week. Is that good for us? Is that good, period?

The issue merits consideration at a number of levels. First up, I am reminded of what the great red bearded gillie said to me, not long since, after one of his gentlemen returned from such an eastern foray. "Tha's hum rooned," said the great red bearded gillie, his great red beard bristling the while. "A hunnert fush tae's ain rod the week. It's rooned, he is. He's nae int'rest in fushing noo. Just catching. Aye." And it's a fair comment. It goes to the very root of our sport.

Why do we fish? Do we fish to eat? At the rate most of connect with fish, we'd better be darned glad we don't because we'd have starved to death long ago. So no. Do we fish to fish? Well, not exactly, I mean, you have to catch one from time to time or it's not fishing after all; it's fly dangling, which isn't really a recognised sport and would be a very silly one if it was. So do we fish to catch fish? Yes, but with a bit of a reservation.

A mate of mine went on such a trip. I can't tell you how many fish he caught in his week, but it was a lot. Dozens and dozens. All between

15lbs and 20lbs odd. Fish to die for. Here. There, they were nothing special. When he came back, he didn't stop talking about it for weeks. Months. He actually became a bit of a Russia bore, if I'm completely honest. Fortunately he recovered. One night, much later, in the wee hours, after a fruitless day on a domestic river, beside a malt bottle that we had almost done to death, I asked him if he missed it? Catching all those fish? Connecting with every other cast? He looked at me long and hard and then stared into the fire and slugged malt. "Fishing," he said, "is about what you are not doing. If you are not catching fish, you dream of fish. If you are catching fish the whole time, you dream of just fishing." And then he passed out.

However I wonder if the possibility, indeed probability, of such large catches of salmon abroad should not prompt other concerns. What, for example, will happen to our own great rivers if anglers are lured away to parts foreign? Who will pay the vast sums necessary to fund the maintenance, investment, improvement – ultimately, the saving – of our own treasures? Why would anyone but a confirmed eccentric, probably certifiably so, pay for the chance to pursue a dwindling resource when abundance beckons a few thousand miles away?

What really concerns me though is the inevitable association of the numbers and the fun. We had a hundred; ergo we had a good time. We got two hundred; therefore we had twice as much fun. Huge mistake. Massive. I shoot a good deal and this is exactly how shooting has got itself in a huge muddle. One bird good, two better, hundreds therefore marvellous. It is not true and it is no truer for salmon than pheasants. "More is better!" is a late 20th century misconception that has no place in fishing or in any other sport.

We fished; we had fun. We caught fish; bonus. We caught 743 fish between five of us in four days. Not interested. Couldn't give a toss. Who cares? Only accountants count. Gentlemen and anglers should enjoy their fishing and their friends and their very occasional fish.

Now this may all sound appallingly pompous and, indeed envious. It probably is; but I warrant that if we once let the joys of fishing become confused with the number of fish that are caught as a consequence of fishing, then the sport, as a sport rather than a business, will atrophy and die. Russia may indeed be the new Eden, but Eden can be mucked up by those enjoying it quite as much as anywhere else. Read the book. Incidentally I'd love to go. For research, obviously. If anyone wants to invite me, I'll be there like a shot; but not, I hope, just to catch a hatful of fish. For the sport.

If you are not catching fish, you dream of fish.

Shades of Granny

My old granny was a bit of a stickler for form. Born with the century, she grew up in a time when people of a certain ilk and age lived pretty much by the do's and don'ts. This stuff was important. Chaps opened doors for ladies and doffed their tile in the street. Ladies didn't drink beer and wore hats with fruit on them. It all seems a bit silly to us these days, but grandpa caught a machine gun burst in the Great War and granny drove a NAAFI three-tonner round the ack-ack sites in the air raids during the re-match, so their entitlement to the moral high ground when it came to proper behaviour was beyond question.

Granny was a great fan of the telephone. Hours and hours. She liked to talk, of course, and the fact that her interlocutor might be miles, hundred of miles, away and busy to boot only made the whole undertaking more exciting still. On and on and on.

It was not unusual to actually leave the receiver on the sideboard and to get on with other stuff, like redecorating the spare bedroom or deadheading the antirrhinums, and simply return from time to time with a judiciously timed "Well-well" or an "Oh really?" or a very occasional "Surely not?" and eventually granny would bring the conversation, if you can call it that, to an abrupt close as she finished her glass of gin-and-it or heard 10 o'clock chime.

10 o'clock was the witching hour. Use of the telephone after 10pm was a sin. Poor form. Or before 10am for that matter. Chaps weren't about and ladies were not decent before 10am in the morning - and after 10pm in the evening a person might be "busy"; though what "busy" involved I, for one, was too discreet to enquire. Anyway, those were the rules and I have, at some subliminal level, lived by them ever since. In an emergency, half and hour either side: house fires, heart attacks, these sort of reasonable exceptions.

So I was startled the other night when the telephone trilled long gone eleven. Trilled? Warbled? What is it exactly that phones do these days? They don't ring, that's for sure. Your mobile may play Beethoven or

Granny was a great fan of the telephone.

the Magnificent Seven, but the landline still sort of warbles. Though no one, as far as I know refers to "Warbling the office" or "Giving the wife a warble". Forget it. The phone went. I was not however "busy", more's the pity. Whisky and the fag-end of *Newsnight*, me. I put aside my glass, muted Paxman, which was a deal more than some weasely government minister had managed, and took up the instrument.

There seemed to be a party going on at the other end. I heard singing and the clink of bottles. Voices raised in laughter. "Sorry to ring so late…." (not warble, you note, *ring*) "but it's quite important." I recognised the tones of my little sister. Well, younger sister. The one who is married to the fishing brother-in-law. He's very firm about fishing etiquette, you will recall, and won't let me on the river without a tie. And her genes have more than a touch of granny about them so a call at this hour was way off beam. I steeled myself for the crisis. The party continued in the background. What crisis? She was in Scotland for week with her husband. A cold sensation began to build in me nethers. "I just had to tell someone……." a chilly fist grabbed a slack handful of vitals. "I've caught a huge fish!"

Blast off! A huge cheer washed down the line from the party in the background. I felt for my glass. I subsided into the hall chair. "How huge?" I whispered, visions of Miss Ballantine swimming before my eyes. "Twelve pounds!" says she. "It's colossal!" Not a record then; but a good bit bigger than my biggest. Twelve pounds bigger, to be exact. First time out. Would you credit it? Her husband taught her to cast and her host pointed her in the direction of a likely spot. She flung her flea and she caught her fish. And they had been partying ever since. And why not? "And, Giles," she added "it was great. I think I know why you boys do this stuff all the time now. I need some waders for Christmas. I'm into this fishing thing. And a tie." A pause. "A tie?" says I. "Of course a tie," she says. "I had to borrow one today. You can't expect to go on the river without a tie. Sorry about the time. " Like I said, Granny's genes not far below the surface. Salmon and women. Could it be true?

On a separate note, I have deliberately not lectured you about the forthcoming Liberty & Livelihood March. This is because I know that you will all be going, to support our fellow sportsmen and to defend their and our essential freedoms from a repressive and deeply untrustworthy government which is at the beck and call of strident and unseemly groups who know little or nothing about little or nothing and care less even than that about you, me or the fluffy cartoon creatures they purport to represent. We will march because we are free, because we are sportsmen and because not to do so would be a betrayal of every generation of sportsmen who should follow us to the quiet places that we love. I shall be there, the little sister will be there; I dare say she will bring her fish with her, certainly the nephews will be along. Not marching would be very poor form anyway.

Fishing, Art & Sex

I once went to a notable art gallery in Vienna. I think it was Vienna; perhaps it was Amsterdam. I can't remember what it was called. So it wasn't really very notable, or at least memorable either for that matter. This isn't really going in the direction I was hoping, is it? Perhaps I'd better start again.

I recall going to an art gallery once. Not something I do often, but there you go. The original Philistine, me. Art-wise. It was somewhere in Europe. Actually I was cajoled into going by a business acquaintance who was a trustee, and something of an expert in these things. We looked at a lot of still life paintings by Dutch Old Masters. You know the sort of thing, a lot of fruit in a basket with the occasional chicken hanging somewhat forlornly from a hook in the background, a chop or twain, and a couple of bread rolls, and, stay with me for this, a brace of fish staring glassily at the viewer from the bottom right hand corner.

All very picturesque, you say, but what has all this got to do with a sporting book? The answer is nothing at all really, except that it leads us neatly into the sex thing. That is what the fish signify. Sex. All those still lifes are allegorical. Everything means something and they are largely on a religious theme, but because being caught painting religious paintings in the Netherlands in whenever the Old Masters were slapping away at their canvases meant an early slot in the decapitation stakes, or perhaps an early stake in the burning queue, the chaps preferred to pretend that they were simply drawing buns and fruit and the odd bass. Those in on the gag however looked at these pictures and saw the heretic old testament laid out before them. It's a bit like those 3-D drawings, where you have to get the right angle before you can get the true shape of things. What a chortle they must have had.

The upshot of which is that fish equals sex. I can't remember quite what the rest means, because I wasn't really listening to my pal as we ambled around the museé, but I'm bound to say that I perked up when we got to the fishing and sex part.

The facts of life.

Because, and this is really the point of the whole thing, sex and fishing are for ever linked in my mind ever since my father took it into his head that a day's fishing with me in tow would be an ideal chance to explain to me the Facts of Life. It took him some time to work up to the subject, and there was a good deal of water flogging, flask tugging and harumphing generally before he would announce "You may have noticed, at certain times of the year…..Oh! Watch it! Line in! Tip up! God save the Queen! Keep the pressure on, for Heaven's sake. Two pounds easily. Gently now!…." And thus it was. Every time the old boy had just about got himself nerved up to do the business. "Marvellous here, isn't it? The birds, the dragon flies. Birds and bees. Yes. Ah. Birds and bees. Yes. Well. You may have noticed….Whoa-ho! We're in. The old Baby Doll. Never fails to get something going in these conditions. Can you fetch the net?" Off we would go again.

I never did discover what the Facts of Life were, or are. Or more to the point, I never discovered what his version was. I seem to have done alright for all that, even if I was something of a late starter as a consequence of having to wait for the fishing season to come round in order that I could find out what to do, and then wait for the season to end before finding time to put theory into practice. And, of course, it took me a number of years to realise that I was never going to get the straight material while there were fish to be had.

I still fish with him today. For all I know he is still trying to nerve himself to the task of letting me in on Life's greater secrets, although given his age now, I dare say the Facts are becoming more difficult to disentangle than a three dropper leader in a gale. More recently therefore we talk, on the bank, of other things, but I'm bound to say that we talk more now than we did then. And that is a positive thing.

On the other hand, I have discovered, by a happy combination of considerable good fortune and diligent efforts on my part, that fishing can deliver a considerable insight into the Facts on its own account. Circumstances must be right, of course; no point going too early in the season. Too cold, and I am not sure about the fishing either. Or too late in the season when there are precious few fish about anyway. But during the lazy, warm, comfortable days of summer, with a good picnic to hand. A loaf of bread, a jug of wine - you know the sort of thing - then there is nothing to prevent a very jolly sort of a day on the side of lake or stream. Nothing so becomes a bloke as the role of successful hunter-gatherer, casting skillfully, forcefully and yet at the same time with an exquisite gentleness and fineness of touch. Meanwhile on the bank there is a blanket, an ice bucket and a plate of olives. Well, put it this way, it works for me. Not invariably, but enough. And that, as any sporting fisherman will tell you, is as near to a limit as you need to be.

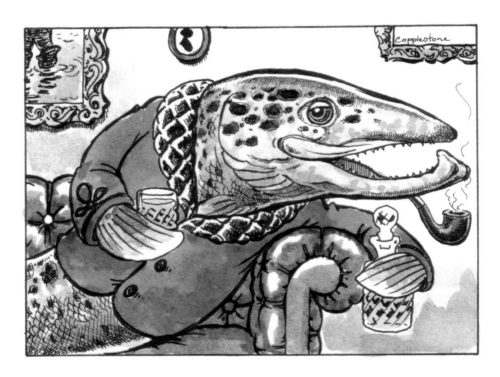

A jolly salmon in a mauve smoking jacket.

Fishing As Viagra

Oysters and stout. We all know what that means. Viagra be damned. Oysters and stout will keep you up all night. Keeps me up all night anyway. Tends to do very little for my sex life, mark you; but sleep, or anything other than a fitful slumber? Oysters and stout will get me every time. And curried oysters and stout? In quantity? And cheese and port? I don't know why they call it the festive tide of Yule. Tidal wave of hurl, more like.

Any road up, I was sitting in bed, staring sightlessly at a diagram purporting to show the proper way to execute a left-handed reverse Spey cast or some such in three easy steps, when the shadows on the sofa by the window seemed to resolve themselves somewhat into a reclining figure. I would have remonstrated. But I wasn't well. The figure disposed itself into a huge and jolly salmon in a mauve smoking jacket. His great face was suffused and a curvaceous pipe dangled from the massive hooked jaw. In one fin he cradled a heavy tumbler and there was a decanter at his side. "Would it be Jock McTangle on the reverse Spey, ye're readin' then?" he says. "Yon glaikit tangler couldn'a hurrl a flea much beyond his ain nose, so he couldn'a. Ma Goad, are they still trying to foller hus wee piccitures? Ma Goad."

I sought to put a degree of haught into my response. "You are familiar with McTangle then?" I said. "Och away you," says the fish, "nae so familiar as old Jock wushed tae git wi' me. I must ha' passed his flea more times than a grilse has lice. Aye, and tugged him the noo; jist for devilment, ye ken?" He lapsed into a contemplative chortle, as he helped himself to another dram. "Aye, we tugged auld Jock noo'n agin, chust to keep his interest, as we passit him by."

The salmon chortled again, his huge belly straining at the elderly velvet of his jacket. "Aye, A've pulled all the big men - and the hairies. All the big fush do it. Part o' the plan, ye ken?" I begged him explain. "Och, the stotters, the glams?" I must have looked as stupid as I felt. "The wimmin? Aye, all the big fish gie the'sel' tae wimmin fishers. It was agreed at the Salmon Council in 1890 as a mark o' respec' for the Queen Empress Victoria. Och, an' as a fine jape on yous fellas an' all. Did ye no guess yet? Ma Goad. Them were days." He looked doleful and slopped another dram into his glass and stared at the bowl of his pipe. "Aye, all gone noo. The big fush. And the big fushers too. The McTangles. Big wimmin. Aye, all gone noo. Christmas past. Ma Goad."

I suppose I must have slept. Which was rude if you like, because when I looked again at the divan the great jolly salmon was gone and in his stead there was a long lean specimen in a threadbare suit that I suspected he had slept in. His skin was blotchy and peeling; his eyes were glazed and filled with mucus; his fins were bent and distorted and as he breathed - gasped, I should say - yellowish bubbles dribbled from his gills. He had a piece of mesh tangled in his jaws and his head was shrouded in a halo of knotted nylon. If I caught his like, or even if you did, we'd put the poor bugger back and hope that no one had spotted us. His voice rasped as he spoke. "No big fish now. Where have all the springers gone? Lost at sea," he said "Lost at sea. Ah me. Ah me." He coughed and a trickle of greenish phlegm ran down his chin. "What on earth" says I "happened to you?"

The salmon laughed a reedy laugh and the flow of bubbles from his gills increased. "What do you think?" he replied. "You. You bastard. You happened to me. With your water abstraction and your hydro-electrics and your damned aggregates extraction and your orgasmo-bloody-phosphate fertilisers and your deep sea drift nets and your loch cages and antibiotic this and macro-biotic that. You and yours is what happened to me and mine." He doubled over on the sofa as a spasm of racking coughs shook his raddled frame. "There's no food in the sea, and there's no peace in the rivers and there's Cymag in the spawning beds and slurry and worse seeping into every stretch of fresh water from Reykyavik to Roehampton. You spend two years at sea looking over your damn shoulder when you should be looking for food; and six weeks back-stroking up some filthy stream spewing your guts out when you should have nothing on your mind but getting laid. You want to try it some time, matey and see how you feel about the whole thing." And then he

140

threw up noisily and colourfully on the carpet. I looked away; and when I looked again he was gone.

I was pretty shaken I can tell you. I went into the bathroom to fetch a glass of water and some aspirin, and as I sluiced my face I thought I heard a tiny voice from the drain. I shut off the flow and listened. "Help us!" it said. I goggled at the sink and listened. It came again. "Help us!" "Help who?" I said. "Us," said the wee voice. "Who is us?" I said. A tiny fry flipped out of the plug-hole and perched on the rim. "We are fry," he said "We are Christmas future. Yours and ours. We are trapped down here because there is nowhere else to go. All the water is in pipes and bottles and we have nowhere to play and live and feed and swim and breed. Help us now or it is the end of your sport and our species." I looked at the tiny fish in wonder. "What should I do?" I asked. The little salmon looked at me long and hard with sad, sad eyes. "Make a difference," he said and dived into the U-bend. I watched the eddy trickle away as I swallowed my pills, but the little fish was gone. I padded back to bed a more thoughtful scribbler and angler and tried once more to sleep.

Yesterday morning the Editor of *Trout & Salmon* called me and asked if I would write a piece for Christmas. "What about?" I asked. "Oh," says he, "I don't know. That's what I pay you good silver for. How about what you want for Christmas?" I pondered. "What I want...," I said and there was a pause while the Editor braced himself, "I want..... to make a difference."

The Editor snorted derisively. "Bah!" he says. "Humbug!" he says. "Alright," he says at last, "As you wish. But I don't see how the Dickens that will make a story."

Sunfishing

I was in Colombia the other day. And before you all start, no I didn't. I wouldn't anyhow, but as a matter of fact the opportunity never arose. So there. Hah! and Pshaw! Not a sniff. So, I was in Colombia. It's not a bad throwaway opening actually, is it? I shall have to remember that.

Anyway, I was staying in Cartagena, which is on the coast in the north of the country, and the surf pounding the golden sands is the Caribbean - which is nice. It is very, very hot and one reason for lolling in the water a good deal is because it is about the only sure way to be anything other than hot too; and horribly, filthy, sweaty hot into the bargain. Fortunately I had a nice air-conditioned hotel room, with a shaded balcony and a swimming pool to boot. Complete with hot and cold, although mainly hot I suspect, staff loitering about in crisp linen just waiting to do one's bidding and fetch the necessary from time to time.

All very well and good, I hear you cry, let's cut to the chase - where's the fish? OK. I was here, or as it was, there, for purposes quite other than fishing, but I had noticed that in one of the hotel's brochures there was mention of sunfishing. Now I have never come across a sunfish before so I was not exactly sure what sunfishing might involve. I mean to say, are we on the water in a dinky little rowboat with a bamboo and a bent pin out the back?; or are we perhaps in a pukka motor boat with one of those swivel chairs on the afterdeck where you strap yourself down with more webbing than a Tornado pilot? Sundry crew-members in singlets and baseball caps spend the next sixteen hours alternately pouring buckets of water over the screaming reel and cans of beer into you as a titanic struggle ensues? Come to that we might very well be in the water as much as on it, with a snorkel and a spear gun. Or perhaps these famous sunfish are desperately rare, and if we are really, really quiet and really, really lucky we might just catch a glimpse of the first one to have been seen by Europeans this century. Damned if I know, and I don't suppose any of you lot is any better.

Now you may well ask why I did not simply breeze up to the nearest crispy member of staff and say clearly and firmly "Now look here, my man, this sunfishing lark? What does it involve and where? One hundred words or less and look sharp about it." The point is that this part of the world happens to be one of the few places which the English have never colonised. Sir Francis Drake floated over the horizon at Cartagena once about five hundred years ago, took a brief look and allowed himself to be bought off for 10,000 pesos, about a quid today, and thought he'd pulled a very fine stroke indeed. Various other pirates, brigands, corsairs and privateers put in now and again but for some reason they never got round to leaving much language behind. Death, destruction, rape, pillage and the pox certainly - but very little conversational English. Nope, it's all Spanish down here; and a pretty ramshackle local version at that. So even if I did speak fluent Spanish, which I don't, I would not have been much better off. Reliant therefore on the two languages I am fluent in, being English and rather louder English, I did make tentative enquiries about the nature of sunfishing. "Oh Si, si senor. Bueno. Good. Muy bueno. Sunfish. Si. Si." Which was about where I left matters for the time being.

In due season my other business being concluded, I signed up for the sunfishing expedition and was shown towards a distant hut on the beach. Much nodding accompanied by "Si. Si. Sunfish." So on arrival I shoved at an open door and ambled into the cool interior. The place was clearly a boathouse, a point somewhat underlined by the neat racks of fibreglass dinghies on the walls and the rows of spars and other gear. There was also a bloke, who looked round and said "Oui, M'sieu." Yes I know it's French and it took me a bit adrift too. "Sunfish," says I. To which he says "Oui. Sunfish." Which did not exactly shed much light on matters. "Sunfishing?" I rejoined smart as a whip, adding a pretty effective rod and line charade for good measure. "Non," says he "These are Sunfish. Sailing boats. But they are 'ow you say, out of service. *En panne.* Having their bottoms scraped."

So there you have it. A Sunfish is a twelve foot fibreglass single handed dinghy which is presumably great fun in the azure waters of the

143

Mare Caribe, but not a lot of help to a bloke who has his mind set on a Hemingway-type adventure, man against marlin, in the sweltering sun and seething surf of the pirate coast. Still these things are sent to try us.

Incidentally when I got home a day or so later, I awarded myself a consolation prize of a trip to the pond. It being the first Sunday of the month there would be a work party which I should really go to anyway, but I would take tackle to be on the safe side.

As it turned out the work party was cancelled, according to the note pinned up in our hut, so with a clear conscience I tackled up and headed off to the sheltered side, for the wind was distinctly chilly, especially after the heat of S. America. I passed one other Rod on my way, who said he'd had one so far, but there seemed to be a hatch of sorts developing, because several black flies seemed to be emerging which were being blown across the water and the trout were snatching them off the surface. So I bunged on a medium sized Black Viva, with a tad of weight just ahead of him on the leader and lobbed him out.

I had scarcely got a ciggy going, as is my wont first thing on the water, when the line went very distinctly tight and then went steaming off across the lake. I won't weary you with details but suffice it to say, after a bit of a struggle, I banked a handsome fish not far shy of three pounds. I was quite chuffed. I cast out again and hadn't even drawn the first pull of my retrieve when we were off again. I popped the second in the bag and tried again. This time I did at least do some fishing before being back in action. I think about three casts. After four fish in the first half hour there was a period of calm. For which I'm bound to say, I was quite grateful.

Don't get me wrong, I'm not against catching fish. Far from it, I know what the bottom line is, but not all at once. Anyway we limit ourselves to three brace a day, so I didn't want to storm through my allowance at quite this pace. It's a fair journey for me to the pond and it would be a less than ideal adventure if I spent less time on the water than I did on the road. Then I caught number five. Well, you know what they say, the last one always takes as long as all the rest put together. And they're right as usual. It must have taken me all of forty five minutes to round out the bag. Just as well I hadn't packed a picnic. Still, who's arguing with six fish in the bag on a speculative venture in some not terribly promising conditions? Not me.

Just over the sea-wall I could see a fleet of dinghies racing upstream towards the bridge. They were fairly buzzing along and the wind was whipping plumes of spray across their decks. It looked a very chilly pursuit indeed, hanging out across the gunwale with your arse in the water this early in the morning, this early in the year. I poured myself a cup of coffee from the thermos. They had a big orange blob on their sails. I'm not sure, but I think that means Sunfish.

You Must be Mad!

I was fishing recently when I was struck by the peculiar absurdity of the whole undertaking. I mean: what is the likelihood of a one inch artificial fly, no more than a hook with a feather attached, being spotted by a twelve inch fish, in 26 acres of water? There's me trying to coax another foot of line out of the rod as I flail back and forth, and for all I know there isn't a fish within a hundred yards. And that's in a stocked trout lake. And yet we do catch something, sometimes; so I suppose there is some truth in the whole theory.

With salmon it is even worse because they have no interest in the fly in the first place. And yet…

I was fishing in Scotland not long ago and it rained the whole of the second day. The following morning we were confronted by a swollen river the colour of tired milky tea. "No point fishing today, I suppose?" our leader (the knowledgeable one) suggested to the gillie. "Och," says he, as gillies will, "Och, ye'll chust have to lash on a bigger flee." So we duly attached the biggest and ugliest lures in the box and began the forlorn flog. And about third dip, Rich connects. A week a year for ever, he's been fishing. Prime weeks every year, on prime beats too and never so much as a tickle. Fifteen years, he says, and not even a tuglet. And now, under conditions described, in every book ever written on the noble art, as being 180 degrees diametrically opposite to ideal or even any good at all; under circumstances when any experienced fisherperson would take one look and withdraw to the nearest hostelry with a fat wallet and a good book; against all the odds; Rich is into a fish.

Not, it must be said, a very big fish, judging by the way it fought. Or more particularly by the way in which Rich reeled him in without anything like a struggle. He made the most he could of it. After all, when you've waited yea long and Lord alone knows how expensively for a fish, you don't just wind it in like an everyday sort of a minnow. So the rod bent and the reel duly screamed from time to time; but not very convincingly when you came down to it. But Rich was having the moment. Well, you can imagine. All those years, all those congratulations he had offered to so many fishing partners. All the gritted teeth and tight smiles. All the girls who had sat on the bank and never beheld him in his neanderthal magnificence, bending Nature to his will with rod and line, hunter-gathering hither and yon. Providing. Forget the receding hairline and the expanding waistline. A man in control. In his element. A MAN. Well, more or less. I expect he was thinking along those sorts of lines. I do. You would. And from time to time he laughed.

And then he banked it. No silver springer this. No lice-bound two sea winter beauty. Neither kipper nor kelt. Not even a salmon. A grayling. And foul hooked into the bargain. And that was what really got to him. That was when the tears came. He's a grown man. Lovely family. Successful in business. A lion in his own patch of jungle. And he sat on the bank with his head in his hands and he wept. Why? Because the river was all of two hundred yards wide and we were fishing a couple of miles of it at least. The water was light brown and the sun was shining. No fish could see an inch let alone a fly. The place was heaving with great big shiny silver salmon. We knew because they were still jumping from time to time to prove it and to irritate us. But had his far flung flee inadvertently snagged the back of a 40lb monster?

Had he hauled a double figure fish up the bank by its tail, Rich would have been properly apologetic, humble even. He might even have put it back. Probably would have; but he would have put it in the book just the same. When the salmon fishers gathered in the bar for a dram and a yarn he would have said "Did I tell you about the time I foul-hooked a forty pounder?" And when the tinies gathered round and pressed his knees, he would tell them, once again, how he had battled the titanic fish which Fortune, rather than his own skill, had granted him.

And yet, and yet, and bloody yet, in all that water, in all those conditions, after all those years and weeks and days and hours of diligence and effort, Rich had been rewarded not by hooking, quite accidentally, the biggest thing in the river bar the railway bridge; but instead had managed to dredge up the smallest catch possible without a diamond set in the middle. And so he wept. And so he might. And so might you. When you think about it, fishing is a patently absurd occupation.

…and foul-hooked into the bargain.

Eat What You Reap

It's a terrible thing getting old. The worst part about it is the insidious creep. I accept that my libido is diminishing at more or less the same rate as my hair; which is fine. This is Nature's way of telling me to slow down. Or perhaps to speed up. Or just knock the whole area on the head right now. Anyway, far worse than this is the occasional sudden revelations that I am becoming my parents, or grandparents. Or worse - other people's parents.

I had one of these moments of revelation only recently. I was shrimping with my nephews, floundering back and forth in the creek up to our middles in the water; pausing from time to time to peer into our nets and to retrieve the little brown shrimps from amongst the seaweed and crabs and sundry flotsam. When, however, I described how much I was looking forward to a spot of shrimp cocktail, the suggestion was met with shrieks of horror. Eat them? Worse still, boil them and eat them?

Boil them, peel them and eat them? "Phoo-yuk-ping!! Uncle Giles. How could you? What a ghastly thought." I'm bound to record that this has little enough to do with scruples, and more to do with a strong aversion to anything approaching work. Sentiments, in general, with which I am happy to say that I agree profoundly, although it goes somewhat against the grain to exercise a catch-and-release policy on shrimps. Accordingly I began to explain how important it was that we should harvest what we could of Nature and that we should always eat what we harvest.

And suddenly I was Uncle Philip of myth and legend and we were sitting in the rain on some Godforsaken Suffolk bog, dangling a maggot in a ditch. Now Uncle Philip is in one way or another responsible for a goodly proportion of my sporting attitudes and approaches and I owe him much. But I have to admit that on the 'eat whatever we catch' issue, Uncle Philip and I fell out more than somewhat.

The day started badly. Uncle Philip wore tweed whatever the weather and whatever the purpose and universally strode about in vigourous bungalow checks. My mother on the other hand took the view that shorts and sandals were an appropriate combo for a growing lad, so that when we assembled for the fishing expedition he was resplendent in Harris and waders, while I wasn't. I won't even attempt to describe how a small boy feels when so completely ill-equipped, but if you think how the donkey feels in the paddock at the Grand National, or more especially the donkey's jockey perhaps, you will begin to have some concept.

In addition to which when we arrived at the river, sorry - canal, rather - dyke, really - ditch, actually - it had started raining. Which meant nothing for Philip, of course, who merely turned up his collar and pulled his flat cap further down over his eyes. But which added a plastic macintosh to my misery. Do you remember plastic macs? A creation more horrible would be hard to imagine. Cold, sticky, inefficient and about as cool as the Sahara. It was not a happy little boy who crouched, cheeks burning with embarrassment and resentment in equal measure, beside the muddy trickle that passed for water.

Notwithstanding which I managed to nail two small perch and a roach. None was bigger than the palm of my hand, which was not a big palm to start with, but when all is said and done, size doesn't matter does it? Let's hold that thought and go home with it, shall we? Anyway, I had a bag and under all the circs. that was enough.

It was not however enough for Uncle Philip. Nothing would do but we cook them on the spot and consume the things fresh. Accordingly we huddled in his dormobile and slapped a frying pan on the gas stove. Butter was melted and the tiny fish cleaned. Then fish were introduced to butter. And promptly leapt out of the pan. What sort of post mortem nervous spasm this was I have no idea, but as we retrieved the tiny cadavers from the floor for the second or third time and Philip held them down with a fork, the smell of slightly burned fish was becoming overpowering. A scent not improved significantly by the company of several wet labradors steaming quietly in the back of the van. As a matter of fact, I came very close to throwing up altogether, and bailed out into the fresh air accordingly. And no, I didn't after all want any of the most delicious fresh fillet of mud either. Thank you.

And so I got the lecture about reaping what you can and always eating what you reap and blah-blah and so on and so forth, and frankly I disagreed, and said that for my money I would have happily thrown the little buggers back and been thankful and sod the harvesting. If not quite in so many words. And I got more lecture, and the dogs got the fish. And Philip got the moral victory, which as a Godfather he was entitled to. But I had the last word, unspoken naturally, when the dogs projectile-vomited an unseemly fishy confection down Uncle Philip's neck in the middle of the journey home.

Having thought over all of which, I agreed with the nephews that emptying the shrimp bucket into a rock pool intensively stocked with crabs, while morally reprehensible, might be extremely good fun.

What's Best for the Guest

I was addressing the issues of riparian etiquette the other day. I know you probably describe it differently – sounding off, perhaps or banging on, or maybe just ranting and frothing; but these things are important. At least to me they are. They give structure and cohesion in an otherwise confused and confusing world. Dear God, I'm beginning to sound like the Home Secretary. Anyway, there is a proper approach and a way of doing things when fishing. A one-two-three and turn and dip. However, I recently found myself in a situation which seemed beyond the familiar territory. And what made the territory all the newer and more alarming was that I was catching fish. Needless to say it didn't start that way.

I had taken Jim as a guest up to the pond. The season was progressing nicely, and it was early summer. The dragon-flies were starting to buzz about the reeds and the occasional startled quacking suggested that some of the ducks were getting broody, and that the drakes were frisky into the bargain. We began on the easy side of the water, casting with the breeze on our backs which made the whole operation considerably easier. There is a depression just off the bank at the bottom end and when the sun is shining, as it was, the trout very often lurk in there where the water is deeper and cooler. I plonked Jim there or thereabouts and issued him with a Viva and a Cat's Whisker to be getting on with, and left him to it.

Now a small digression. You will doubtless have noticed that I just referred to a couple of flies by name. I might have just plucked these names from a book, or from the catalogue that fell out of last month's copy of *Trout and Salmon* As it might be a Black and Peacock Spider, or a Teal Blue and Silver; or perhaps a Patagonian Tufty Red Throat. I might even be making them up as I go along; most people wouldn't spot the difference. But, but, but it's really true; I *do* know these flies. They are the killer flies on this water and after much diligent training I am in a position confidently to pick them out of the box. I always take one of each because I'm still not 100% on which is which, but this I tell you – one is black and the other white, and if one doesn't get you a tug, then the chances are that the other will.

Jim promptly got a take on the black one – thus demonstrating that he too is no expert on the minutiae – and shortly thereafter landed a tidy fish. Not twenty minutes later and he was in action again, and again he deftly netted a decent specimen. This is very satisfactory progress, thinks I, watching indulgently. Always good to see the guest getting stuck in, even if I haven't had so much as a tug. Things went very quiet for a couple of hours then, and by lunchtime the score remained 2-0.

After a sandwich and a beer I decided that I would try the other side of the water. There is a promontory on the far side, which meant that I would not be casting into the wind, and I just yearned for different ground to cover, since I was manifestly doing no good where I was. Jim decided to stay where he was for the nonce, since he had pulled two there and he is a creature of habit after all. So we parted company and I took the long stroll.

I lashed on the Cat's Whisker (it's the white one I am advised) and put a split shot some two foot from the end of the leader on a floating line. It may be heresy but I like to think that the fly is getting some depth. The fish, after all, are in the water, so the lure should be too. Third cast and BOOMPH! Lots of fight and much zooming hither and yon, but the fish was on the grass betimes and a goodly fish at that; tickling three pounds I shouldn't wonder and that's good for us. Two casts later and another went into the bag after the first. I got a tickle only minutes later and a third fish, from the exact same spot, shortly after that. At which point Jim, having seen the rod tip bending betimes arrived at a canter and parked himself next to me. He too lashed on a Cat's Whisker and he too added a little weight. He cast in the exact same spot. And I caught another. He cast again. I cast again. He cast again. I caught another. At which point my nice point arose. What is the correct behaviour for a host who is catching fish while his guest, with identical set up and within casting distance of the same water, catches nothing? We swapped places – I caught a fish. We swapped rods – and when I picked his up, it had a fish on. We swapped flies, hats, glasses and flasks. I caught fish; he just fished. Eventually I just stopped fishing. No, no, no, no, no, much too exhausted. Too, too exciting. Enough is as good as a feast. Press on, why don't you? Last one's yours. I'll just sit here and have a smoke break.

Well, I could have smoked myself to a crisp for all the good it did. To add to all our difficulties, another angler joined us in the vicinity and Lo! He killed four fish in short order. And still Jim couldn't connect. Eventually he was giving off as much smoke as I was, what with effort and frustration – oh and sunburn. Finally he passed me the rod "Dammit! Dammit! What do I have to do?" he cursed. "Just reel him in," I said and passed the rod back. I kid you not, it was that quick. The question is what do you do in that situation? As a fisherman and a gentleman. Fisherman, anyway. Someone must know. Please?

It opens our eyes to the beautious rhythms of nature…

Fishing Lies

So the young and shiftless and idle and disaffected and criminally inclined are going to be sent fishing. They should fit right in then.

The government is endorsing, with not insignificant amounts of money and in conjunction with the police, a scheme to take truants fishing when they should be at school. The plan, it is reported, is to get persistent miscreants, or boys, or more especially youths, I expect, out of stressful situations – like classrooms, for example – and off street corners where they are inclined to fall in with the wrong sort and get into all kinds of mischief. Street cricket springs to mind or the sort of misdirected footy kickabout that leads to international superstardom, £60,000 a week, supermodel girlfriends and a silly hair-do. "We want to catch them before they get into criminal habits," says PC Mick Watson, though whether he is referring to indolent schoolboys or recalcitrant carp is not made clear from reports. And, to be honest, the idea of a couple of delinquent tench loitering in some slack backwater slyly talking a gullible trout and some easily misguided young roach from a lakeside care home into boosting the weir on behalf of Mr "Snapper" Pike is too charmingly bucolic to miss.

Now on the one hand I don't want to deride the concept too much because at bottom, perhaps with a ledger rig and some boilies or a sinking line and a trail of nymphs, the idea is perfectly sound.

Fishing is, after all, fundamentally good for you. It does have a calming influence. It does teach you the virtues of iron self-discipline. It imbues the fisherman with patience and a growing regard and respect for his quarry. It opens our eyes to the beauteous rhythms of nature in all its forms. It helps us to learn about a proper restraint in defeat and humility in victory. And it teaches us how to lie consistently through our teeth.

And this is why I have some concerns about the whole project. Fishing is founded on deception. The bait, the lure, the fly, the spoon – the hook – is disguised to take ruinous advantage of the somewhat restricted brainpower and overwhelming hunger of the fish.

We lie to the fish from the off. Fishing is all about the con. The scam. It is the art of deceit writ large. And if it were only the fish that felt the sharp end of the barb it might be forgivable; but fishermen lie to everybody.

We lie to our spouses, partners, families and households. "I'm just going for an hour or so, honestly," we say as we set off shortly after lunch, secure in the knowledge that if there should be a decent hatch come the eventide, it will be midnight before the lintel sees our wadered tread again. Unless the sea-trout beckon, when it will be breakfast. We lie to each other. All the time. The classic caricature of the fisherman is with arms outstretched to imply the size of the one that got away. Has anyone, ever, returned from a pool without claiming to have rolled one?

Most importantly though, we lie to ourselves. Always. One more cast, then, one more and that's it. One more. OK. Change of fly and then one more. If this one doesn't work, we'll change and try just one more.

We are lied to by all and sundry. "Och, ye shuid ha' bin here last week. The watter wass perfect. Issa wee bitty low noo," as the great red bearded gilly greets me every time I venture to the river. The whole undertaking is a series of more or less elaborate charades founded on a long and noble history of deceit, misinformation and chicanery. Should we really be teaching this to impressionable boys? If they are falling in with the wrong company on street corners, I hesitate to think whom they will be falling in with on the banks of lakes, rivers, meres and streams

around the place. Most of us doing the falling in up and down the country started fishing by bunking off school in the first place and now we just bunk off work instead and spend our days lying in the long grass with a cooling glass and flicking a fly now and again. And falling in.

I'm also concerned that the scheme seems to be exclusively male in its approach, both as to its subjects and its supervisors. Where are the ladies in all this? Why are girls not to be introduced into the gentle art of the angle? We all know that they are far better at it than boys anyway, or are they just considered to be too honest? Or too diligent? It's true that we daren't have too many honest and diligent people cluttering our sport. That would upset the whole applecart. Perhaps that is what the government is after. The phased, secret introduction of honesty and integrity into fishing. Oops! There goes the neighbourhood.

A Good Turn at the Fishing Hut

It never rains but it pours. Actually this is not true. It is by way of being an aphorism. It often rains and doesn't pour; but that is when you are looking through the window and wondering whether you might as well make a dash for it because it is only spitting. It pours when you have just begun the dash. Then it fairly lashes down. Until you arrive at the other end of the mad sprint; whereupon it stops. That's the real point. It never pours, but when you're in the middle of it. Bad luck doesn't just graze you; it smacks you right between the eyes and then when you are down and rolling about in pain, bad luck proceeds to give you a good kicking.

I saw this in action only the other day. I was fishing down at the pond. Lovely day. Sunshine, blue sky, nice ripple; but then this isn't about the weather is it? Unless a massive and downwardly mobile slurry flurry can be described as a storm. There is a word for it, but I shall spare your blushes.

On the next pontoon there was a fisherman, a fellow rod. We had "Hello"-ed as he came along the bank, and "Tightlines"-ed as he passed my spot, and during the course of the past several hours I had watched him net a couple of decent looking fish; and, I dare say, he had watched me do the same. At which point Fate definitely took a hand.

The first element of disaster was that his top section flew off. Well, it happens, doesn't it; from time to time? One second you are casting perfectly happily, and the next flop-splosh. The last time it happened to me was at the Game Fair, as a matter of fact. In the double handed distance casting competition. Not that I expected to win, you understand, but I do like to take part. I don't even mind making a modest prat of myself, and can joke about it with the judges and timekeepers. What I do not expect, as a rule, just as I am working line out for a major flail, is for the top half of the rod to fly off behind me on the backcast, catch me on the neck as I hurl it forward once more, and finally to drape me in several yards – though not a prize winning quantity – of loose line. But we are not talking about me.

Well, it happens doesn't it?

Anyway, my neighbour lost his top section on the outcast and it duly flopped into the water ten feet from the end of the pontoon. "No problemo," says you, "just haul in and the fly will catch in the top ring." Yes, but as he was reeling in, a fish hits him. So now he's playing a fish with half the rod in hand and half in the drink. And that's no way to play a frisky fish, as we all know. And it breaks the leader. So now he's got no fly to catch the ring. So as he reels in, the line slides onto the reel and the top section stays where it is. Bobbing about. So obviously he goes after it with the net. And as he's splashing about with the net his glasses drop off his nose, bounce once on the edge of the pontoon and sink into six feet of water.

Well, he got the top section after several minutes, and for the next half an hour I watched him trawling back and forth along the pontoon with the net with no discernible result. After which he flung all his kit into his creel and stumped off back to the hut.

I suppose it was twenty minutes later that I heard the car alarm. And about five minutes more before I ceased thinking about it as an unruly disruption of my personal tranquility and wondered if all was well at the hut. Lunch beckoned in any case so I ambled off.

He was sitting on the bench by the hut with his head in his hands, the motor blaring away a few yards off. What, says I, has transpired now? Well, the long and the short of it was this. He'd stormed up to the hut in a major paddy as you can imagine and weighed in his fish and scratched a curt note in the log. Whereupon he locked the hut, flung his gear in the boot of the car, slammed it shut and realised that not only had he locked the hut keys in the hut, but he had locked the car keys in his jacket pocket in the boot. At which point he kicked the bumper and set the alarm off. Then he wept.

At which point I turned up.

And is there a happy ending? Of course there is. I had a key to the hut, so opening that was the work of a moment and we retrieved his key. The hut also yielded a length of fence wire which (and I shouldn't really tell you this but I was taught it by a chap from the RAC, rather than a mis-spent youth, and it has allowed me to show off wildly on a couple of occasions since) meant that we were into the car a couple of minutes later. After which is was only a matter of folding down the back seats to get the jacket and that was the car keys recovered to, or rather from, boot.

By now, of course, I was this chap's best friend in all the world, in the universe, in space and he was effusive in his thanks as he finally departed.

After my lunch I wandered down to the pontoon where he had been fishing and even as I stepped onto the planking I caught a glint in the water. Keeping an eye on the spot I knelt down and there were the specs just poking through the silt. One sweep of the net and that was that. I noted his address against the list of car number plates our bailiff keeps in the hut for reference and popped them in the post the same evening with a note scribbled on the back of a business card. And two days later I received in the post a very handsome fly wallet and yet more effusive thanks.

All of which goes to show that it never rains but it pours. And that, in the land of the pouring rain, the man with the umbrella can afford to be generous - it may even pay dividends.

They Also Serve

Guess what? I picked up a prize at the Game Fair. Picture in the paper and everything. Not the Game Fair where all the pros go to pick up their trophies but a much more modest affair where the locals pitch along out of the backwoods in the vicinity to collect their postal orders and a free bag of flies. Mark you, I didn't actually win the damn thing. I was mooching round the stalls in the blistering July heat wondering whether the sheepskin seconds staff might be ready to do a deal or if the purveyors of Extra Thick Woolly Jumpers (None Warmer!) might be ready to make their first sale of the weekend, when my mobile phone warbled; as they do.

When I eventually extracted the machine it informed me that I had a text message. It said "U av txt!" which I took to mean that I had a text message, being, as I am, no stranger to the finer points of modern technological jargon. Unscrambling the thing was another matter altogether, of course, but having cornered a passing teenager for the purpose, a message from my elder nephew emerged. Recalling that he had been at the Fair earlier but had left to go sailing instead of waiting for the bargain hour like his wily old uncle I imagined that he wanted me to buy him something. That being the normal function of uncles at Game Fairs. Not a bit of it. "Can u c if ive wun the casting?" it, or perhaps he, asked.

So, off I tootled to Fisherman's Row where I duly accosted the good folk at the Salmon & Trout Association who were hosting the competitions. A lady ran a nail down the lists. "H'm, let's see," says she,

Replying took care of the next half an hour.

"Here he is. First equal, salmon distance, 16 and under. There's a while to go though, so you'll have to come back at 5.00pm." This presented a number of issues. First up was what was I going to do for the next couple of hours? Not loiter about in Fisherman's Row, that was for sure. I can spend a lot of money in a few minutes down there once the retail frenzy gets going, let alone a couple of hours. Secondly, I would have to rethink my exit strategy from the Fair because while it is not so great a show as the CLA, if you leave at the same time as everyone else, you are going to spend a goodly time queuing for the gate. And finally, and more to the point, what was my nephew doing as joint leader of the salmon distance casting competition? With a distance I may add of 28 yards which is better than I can do with a following wind. And he's ten years old. The phone warbled.

"wel?" it said. Replying took care of the next half an hour anyway. "You are lying equal first for the time being. More news later. Who has been teaching you?" The spelling may be well off beam but there is no one to touch him for pace. The reply came back before the phone was back in the pocket. "cool! dad + uncle pete."

Dad, by the bye, is the brother-in-law whose rods and so forth I have occasionally borrowed for forays described here and Uncle Pete is the kid's godfather who has a nice piece of water into the bargain thereby demonstrating the importance of choosing your children's moral and spiritual guardians with the greatest of care.

At the appointed hour I returned to Fisherman's Row. Once more I accosted the lady of the lists and once more she "H'm-ed…" and ran her nail down the columns. "Yes" she says "he's still first equal. Who are you, anyhow?" I said that I was the boy's uncle. "Oooh," she says, "are you the uncle with the nice piece of water who taught him how to cast?" With as much haught as I could reasonably muster I explained that I was the other uncle, without the nice piece of water, who collected prizes on my nephew's behalf. "I see," she says "you're the one who writes a bit and can't cast for toffee then?" That, I said, making a mental note that certain small boys would benefit from the occasional flogging, would be me. "Just wait there then," she goes on, "the prize-giving will be going ahead shortly as soon as the photographer arrives."

Which is how, dear reader, I came to be beaming out of the local paper a few days later, clutching my prize of a travelling coffee mug, as the proud (joint) winner of the Boys (16 and Under) Salmon Distance Casting Competition at the Game Fair. And a very handsome mug it is too. And it doesn't need polishing. I'll give it to the lad when he gets back from Scotland where he is fishing with his dad and his rather more useful uncle who has quite a decent piece of water. I'd text him to tell him I've got it safe if I could remember how the phone works, but knowing him he's probably too busy catching fish to care.

Some kids have all the luck.

Avuncularity Consultant

Drawing as we are again towards the festive tide of Yule, one is confronted by a very particular series of problems which do not diminish over time and are no easier to resolve each year when they swing round with all the relentless regularity of Poet's pendulum.

The first issue is where to spend Christmas. Now I am not some elderly dowager who plonks herself on some poor benighted relative at the last minute with a retinue of dozens and holds court for weeks while complaining about the state of the linen. Nor, on the other hand, am I a dutiful son who spends Christmas with his Mum and Dad diligently unwrapping socks and relishing the cremated turkey. I am the wandering stag. I am the avuncularity consultant.

Family Christmas, when all is said and done, can be a bit of a grim affair. The family who have diligently avoided each other for the better part of a year assemble in one place for one day. By the time lunch, in all its glory, is on the table parents have had enough of children, the in-laws are at one another's throats, the children are fractious and insanely jealous of their siblings' presents, granny is dangerously close to overdoing the amontillado, the matriarch (who has been cooking since six) is at the end of her tether and the paterfamilias has retired to the potting-shed with a bottle of claret and a foul mood. Rancour and family schism beckon.

Enter the avuncularity consultant. The courtesy uncle. He sets up the trainset with skill honed over many years. He has a satchel of batteries which fit any known gadget and gizmo. He issues forth presents to all and sundry which are risque and wildly inappropriate. He amuses and diverts. He takes all the children for a brisk walk. He can peel a spud and mix a martini with equal facility. Most important of all he is not, strictly speaking, family; which means that everyone has to be on best, or at least better than normal, behaviour because you don't air the family laundry in front of guests, after all. There are certain things which parents can never do for their children. They can't teach them to cast, to shoot, to drive or to build a space station without losing half the pieces. Who has not heard

...rancour and schism beckon.

the plaintive cry - not least at this time of year - "It's mine and I want to do it my way! Leave me alone!" Sinatra has much to answer for. Throw an avuncularity consultant into the mix, however, and the kids are prepared to listen, a bit. After all the avuncularity consultant is not a parent. He is different. He has an eccentric motorcar. He spends most of his time on holiday. He shoots like a god. He is not above slipping the whoopee cushion under granny's chair. He knows all the answers. If you are a kid, you co-opt the avuncularity consultant onto your team before the parents get a look in. And then he pushes off on Boxing Day, before any of this stuff wears off. And moves on.

Accordingly my Christmas tends to be peripatetic. A couple of days here. A day there. Christmas day there. Boxing Day shooting somewhere; one of my favourite shoots of the year. A few more days somewhere else and then down to the seaside for New Year. This has become a fixture in the calendar since I have, by a process of osmosis almost, become the official village pyrotechnician. It began with the boatman clearing up the quay and burning some of the wrecks from the autumn storms. I let off a few fireworks and in short order the whole proceedings became a tradition. He builds a huge bonfire on the quayside which is ignited at about 11 o'clock. He rings a bell at the witching hour, whereupon I light the fuse and run for it. There follows five minutes of aerial mayhem with sparks and bangs 'Ooohs!' and 'Aaahs!' and then it is home to a large whisky and heavensent thanks that we have survived to see another dawn.

Whereupon the Boys' Team (of myth and legend) descend for the first shoot of the New Year. They come bearing prodigious gifts of food and drink having abandoned their families for the time being and are determined to do nothing for the next several days but drink good claret, shoot some pheasants and eat anything except cold turkey.

The second big problem of Christmas, of course, is where to begin.

170

Time and Plaice

Summer's lease is ended; but as we sit re-organising the dry flies and sipping a contemplative aperitif of an earlier and earlier evening it is agreeable to revisit the singular triumphs of the balmy days of summer. And singular is almost what they have been.

The pond on which I fish has not had a good season. For one reason and another I have not been able to get there as often as I would have liked. By the time I did make it to the bankside the dreaded weed had put in its triffid-like appearance and it was next to impossible to get a fly through the floating mat into the water. And once there things were little better. Early excitements turned out not to be takes by some over-wintered leviathan but repeated bundles of trailing greensward with the remains of a lure embedded somewhere in the midst of the slimy mess. Followed by shocking infestations of algae. I dread to think what it did to the fish, but it certainly took the gloss off the days I visited. No one had so much as a nibble during the dog days.

With luck the cooler days of autumn will see the water clearing to some extent and perhaps we will have unexpected successes now that we are approaching what used to be the closed season. The fishing will not be so comfortable by any means and the aspect of the place, which is most congenial in the warm summer days with the dragon-flies buzzing about and the pigeons swooping and clattering in the trees, will not be as tranquil, but if we get on terms with some fish finally much else can be forgiven. I shall have moved much nearer to the water, geographically speaking, in the interim which has been one of the things keeping me occupied lately, so more frequent visits will be on the cards. And as the great red-bearded gillie always says "Ye'll no catch a bug fush wi' yer flee in the box!"; so we must hope that more time on the water puts more fish on the bank.

On the other hand the summer was not without its excitements. My new role as avuncularity consultant has taken up considerable time. You will recall how I was gulled into buying a rod by a nephew last year?

171

Well, it's been a roaring success, of course, and the tackle has been given a serious workout this summer. Goodbye Game-Boy and PlayStation II. Hello tiny spinning rod and a pocketful of lugworms. "Where are you going now? It's nearly breakfast/lunch/tea/supper time?" "I'm going fishing with Uncle Giles." "Oh, alright then. Don't be too long." If I heard it once I must have heard it fifty times, and what is a poor avuncularity consultant to do, except lever himself out of a comfortable chair, stick the crossword in one pocket and a can of beer in the other and plod off in the wake of a young angler?

And he's come on in leaps and bounds, I must say. When the little rod first put in an appearance casting was something of an issue. Lots of vim and vigour, to be sure, but we all know where that leads, don't we? Trees and fences. And the occasional bush. Or for the coastal angler rocks, ears and anoraks. And a periodic splosh about three feet in front of the said coastal angler followed by a vicious curse fit to colour the cheek of a sheltered uncle. This year, au contraire, it was a flick of the wrist, a long sizzle and a distant splash on the other side of the estuary. But of quarry not a jot. We tried lug and prawn. We tried spinners and lures. We tried silver paper and the plastic beads which the old bloke who was fishing on the nearby tidebreak swore blind would do the trick. Nothing. Nada. Zip. Zilch. Nulles points.

Finally I went to the fly box and found in the bottom an old bug. Lord knows what it was intended to represent. It had googly eyes and a lot of green tinsel and some smooth-talking tackle emporium salesman had sold it to me in a desperate moment. I guess it was a replica fry of some description. You probably have one too. It looked like a frog with a thyroid condition. We lashed it on and heaved it in. Not much changed.

Then his little mate, who was staying, asked if he could have a try and was duly handed the rod. "Everyone must share," you see, that's avuncular stuff alright. The little mate cast out. Three feet. Splosh. Wallop! Rod bends double. Boys yelling. Uncle pouring beer down his front and setting fire to the crossword with dropped ciggy. Everybody running round shouting. Furious winding. And there it was on the

Flounder. Plaice. Sole. Whatever. Who cares?

beach. Flounder. Dab. Plaice. Sole. Whatever. Who cares? A flatfish. Pound and a half easy. Flapping about on the pebbles with little boys trying to belt it with a rock and Uncle Giles trying to get the cigarette end out of his shirt front. Mayhem.

Was ever a fish so proudly carried home? I doubt it. I was worried though. After all, the nephew had laboured long and hard for a fish and his mate had nailed one first crack out of the box. Life really isn't fair. Fishing really isn't fair. I felt for him, really I did. That's what avuncularity consultants do. So I tried to explain how these things work. He looked at me as if I was mad. "It's OK Uncle Giles," says he, "I don't mind. That's fishing." I was about to applaud these noble sentiments when the little brute went on "Anyway it's my fish as much as his. After all, I told him where to put it. And he owes me an ice cream for the rod hire."

The lad will make a fisherman yet. And a consultant, probably.

Trout and the Art of
Motorcycle Maintenance

Why is fishing important? Why do we fish? What's it all about? Here's an example of why fishing is central to improving the general quality of life for anglers and those around them. It's the week before Easter. The sun has unexpectedly burst forth and the blossom is blossoming. Birds sing, lambs gambol and all is well with the world. I have done a whole bunch of chores, finished a lot of boring correspondence and am in a mellow mood. Time to go fishing, right? Wrong.

The motorcycle has a flat tyre. On the back. No wind whatever. Pancake. Now on a car this would not be critical because somewhere in a car there generally lurks a spare wheel which, with a certain amount of sweat and toil, can be attached in place of the faulty corner and progress can duly be made. On a bike this is not so. We don't carry spare wheels. Still, generally speaking, it is not a critical issue. Stick a bit of air into the wheel and ride slowly and carefully to local friendly bike shop where they mend or replace tyre, fill it with air and send you on your merry way. Was there ever a time when life was like this? A golden age?

There isn't a pump about the place for openers. And we are talking about the middle of nowhere here, after all. So I borrow a car from a neighbour and head for the nearest garage. They do have a foot pump so I borrow that and head back, but before I leave I just want to make sure that if I return in due season with the bike that they will be able to help me out. Just as well I checked. "Normally, sir, yes; but our bike man is off sick today and he's the only one who can manage bikes. Not to worry there's a tyre shop in town who will help you. No worries." Fine. I promise to return the pump in a bit and drive home. Return the car and apply pump to flat tyre. Pump. Pump. Pump. Just enough to get to town before the air runs out. Slowly and gently I go to town and arrive at the tyre shop just as the handling is getting seriously wonky. Can they fix it? "Oooooh-er!" Much sucking of teeth. "Well, normally we could. In fact we can. But we are not allowed to. Health and Safety says that

No wind whatever. Pancake.

bikes are a specialist job and we are not allowed to take the wheel off. Or more particularly, we are not allowed to put them back on for you. We can mend the tyre, but we can't touch the wheel. I think that the other place in town can though. We'll put some more air in it for you so you can try there." More air and another gentle, gentle, nip and tuck trip to the next shop. Can you help? "We used to do bikes, for sure, but our insurers say that the risks are now too great and so we have had to stop. There's a bike shop in the next town though. They could help." Can we call first? "We don't know the name actually. But it's next to the bank. It's only a dozen miles or so. We'll put in as much air as the tyre will take and you can try them."

As you can imagine, I am by this time beginning to lose my sense of mellow springtime-ness. There followed a highlight in a day that was noticeably bereft of highlights. Half way between towns and with a mounting wonkiness developing in the handlebars, I was just contemplating stopping for a pump-pump session when I saw an RAC van about to pull out of a side road and flagged him down. I'm a member after all and I was in the throes of a motoring emergency. Now this is not an ad for the RAC but when I explained the problem this good man said he could mend it on the spot. Not a perfect mend, he was obliged to say, but enough to keep the air in for the time being so that I could ride safely, at modest speed, until I found someone to do a proper job. And he did. Was I happy? Delirious. Was I now relaxed? Considerably more than I had been a few minutes before. We parted with salutes and salutations. Then life started going downhill again. First shop didn't do tyres. Restore you an antique motorcycle, but of modern tyres not a hint. More miles and second shop didn't have the right machine. More miles and third shop couldn't possibly fit me in until a fortnight after Easter. My last stop on this tour of the eastern counties, and I had been on the road for four hours so far, was my local garage to return their foot pump. The first person I encountered was the bike man who was supposed to be off sick who, feeling somewhat improved, had decided to pitch up for the afternoon. Of course he'd fix it. I thanked him through gritted teeth.

So where is the fishing? What's the deal here? You can imagine

- at least if you close your eyes and charge head first into a wall several times, you can - what my mood was by this juncture. I was due out to dinner where I was expected to sparkle charmingly for my supper and where gritted teeth and rolling eyes were scarcely going to cut the mustard.

There was nothing for it. I strapped on rod and creel and rode, gently and sedately obviously, to the pond and spent three glorious, warm, successful hours fishing with a westering sun at my back and trout taking advantage of an early hatch to my front. As I slid the net under a handsome three-pound overwintered fish I shrugged off the travails of the day and drank deep from the well of piscatorial satisfaction and my soul was soothed. My teeth unclamped and my eyes stopped rolling. I took the trout, cleaned and bagged, as a gift for my hostess' freezer and I duly sparkled my way through the evening.

And that, gentle reader, is why we should all fish; because it makes a lousy world a better place.

Crabs again...

Now here's a thing; have you ever caught crabs? Whoa! Ow! Blimey! Gerroff! Let me rephrase the question – have you ever been crabbing? Fishing is fishing in my book and one should never let one's horizons be diminished by mere snobbery. No, it is. It's just snobbery.

So there we were at the seaside. It's the Spring Bank Holiday and I should be up to my middle on the Tweed, or the Helmsdale, or the Naver or whatever, doing some rigorous investigation into the season's prospects for *Trout & Salmon* readers across the globe. Sacrificing a rare week-end, when I could be gardening, or painting the fence or redecorating the spare room, for the benefit of you lot by selflessly flogging sparkly water and banking great shiny silver fish with the resigned air of the truly hardened professional scribbler. I should cocoa.

Instead of which I am standing on the quay with the nephews chasing crabs. Nor are these even edible crabs. Those come from the pots off Cromer. The great red and blue monsters that come dressed or undressed according to taste on the menu or on the winkle cart down by the pier. I'm not mad keen on them myself I have to admit. Too strong for me. And have you ever seen the sort of stuff they eat? If you went crabbing you would. Now a lobster I can get involved with. As long as I don't allow myself to remember how old they are. Did you know that lobsters are elderly? I can't remember exactly how you can tell and, if I guess, there will doubtless be a great cascade of critical correspondence saying how thick I am and how irresponsible it is to mislead the public in this cavalier way and so on; but I believe that it is about a centimetre a year. Would that be about right? So that the little one per person type lobby that you get these days would be ten years old. And a big banquet style centre-piece (many Oohs and Aahs) four or five pounder at two-foot long will be nearly seventy, maybe more. I can't eat things which have lived longer than I have. Unless I'm very drunk. Which is a feature of lobster dinners.

The ideal combo is lobster and Black Velvet - Champagne and Guinness - but good champagne. Don't be cheap about it or it's wasted. And cold; seriously cold. I find that the whole operation is best done out- of-doors as a matter of fact. We do a late summer lobfest, about September, when the evenings are warm and the lavender scent hangs heavy on the air. Split lobsters grilled momentarily on the barbeque with hot tarragon and garlic olive oil. The tail meat you can fork out easily enough, but the claws are best laid on the cobbles and belted with a champagne bottle. Fishy water squirts in all directions and shards of lobby shell whistle about like shrapnel – which is why it is better done outside. The dry cleaning bill for the dining room curtains can be a shocker otherwise.

Anyway,this did not set out as a treatise on how to eat lobster, fun though it is; but as an explanation of the crabbing experience. And the key thing about crabbing is to have a more disgusting lure than the crabber on the pitch next door. In the crab pots I hauled up in Alaska we were using seal heads as bait. Down on the quay it is actually bacon for the most part. Although the best bacon is the stuff that we were using at the end of last summer, and which has spent the winter gently decomposing in a bucket at the back of the boat house. This proves utterly irresistible to the crabs who fling themselves on the porky remains from all parts from the creek. Three and four at a time we are heaving the shiny green brutes up the wall and into the bucket. From babies the size of pennies to serious grown ups as big as your fist; just clinging by a pincer to the abominable bacon.

At first, of course, the tinies are all over the place with excitement. "Ooh, Uncle Giles!! I've got one. Another one. More." But gradually the enthusiasm fades. As the evening chill comes on and the tide laps around our feet finally driving us back from the stony edge of the quay where the best crabbing is to be had, their thoughts turn easily towards ice creams and hot baths and fishfingers and all the other myriad of things which keep little boys occupied.

Which is why as the twilight deepens with the tide you can see the line of wellied uncles still lobbing their bacon into the tide. For when all is said and done, fishing is fishing whatever the quarry, and you don't go home until you have had a last cast.

Rod rage… that's where we were heading.

A Point of Etiquette

I was standing on a street corner the other day, as you do, watching for a gap in the traffic in order to make a mad dash to a traffic island in the middle, in a brave effort actually to achieve a total crossing of the thoroughfare before lunchtime, when I saw a road rage incident. Actually it was less of a road rage incident than a kerb rage incident. This was the sequence of events: first, bloke pulls out of parking meter bay; second, another bloke immediately indicates and pulls up to reverse-park in said bay; third, next car in traffic jam dives nose first into parking slot with arse end hanging out and wiggles to the best that can be achieved under the circs. about three feet from the kerb; fourth, words are exchanged, short Anglo-Saxon and to the point; five, traffic snarls up big time and I am able to sidle between steaming cars and frothing drivers to my luncheon appointment. Why did the chicken cross the road? Probably because it saw the chance, which comes but fleetingly in a chicken's life, and grabbed it.

What has this got to do with fishing? Politeness. Etiquette. Rules written and unwritten. Respect. No. I am quite serious. I know that I am regarded as reliably shallow and facetious; and I am. But I trust that I am never rude. I know that the Aged Parent is instructing his solicitors even as we speak over some imagined slight in a piece here to do with drink, sex and trout; but that is a quite different kettle of, well, fish, and has nothing to do with politeness. It's just to do with complex generational relationship shifts and finding an excuse that the other Aging Parent will accept so that he and I can sneak off together to the pond. I can't go into it all here, but I probably will one day.

Anyway, etiquette, politeness and rod rage. That's where we were heading. First, invitations. Now I happen to believe that invitations should veer towards the formal. I don't get many letters – except from the Gas Board, and very colourful they are to be sure – so it is always nice to get a note saying "Come fishing or, come shooting." I know that the electric telephone has all but abolished the written word, but so

Where were they dragged up?

what? What goes around, comes around. Also a letter permits reflection and consideration, rather than the knee jerk acceptance which is the spontaneous response of the terminally sad. But the note itself should say more than just "Come shooting or fishing." Does the invitation mean come and stay? Here? Or there? If your friends happen to own great tracts of double banks on this great river or that, and you are accustomed to tooling up to the castle and having the under-butler grab your cases and take them to your usual room – then bully for you. But if you are staying in the hotel, or as it might be pub, or for example we just assumed that you would be bring your own tent because we always do, then it is as well to know what you are expected to contribute – especially in terms of paying the bill. There is nothing worse than thanking your host warmly for a wonderful week and his extensive and remarkable generosity and then being presented with your "share" of the outgoings. Clarity and candour then. Up front about who is fronting up. There's the key.

Now my brother-in-law is very agreeable and often takes me fishing. More than this, he lends me most of the gear that I then fish with. And he is very proper about respecting the river and the fish. You do not, for instance, amble down to the river in jeans and a T-shirt. Salmon may not be able to tell a well-dressed fly from a hole in the ground, but they can spot a missing tie at a hundred paces, apparently. And they don't like it. So if you can't dress for the river – forget the whole idea. Now I thought he was bonkers to begin with, but actually he's quite right. It's a respect thing. Your quarry is a noble beast. And you can't expect him to pitch in and make your day if you are slovenly in approach and demeanour.

Then there are the others on the bank. Or perhaps on the other bank. Of course one is polite to the gillie, boatman or bailiff. These boys have all the answers. Rubbing them up the wrong way is just salmon suicide; fishing folly. Do as you are told and don't offer too many opinions. And call them Mister. They have a position in life. I know there are scruffy bundles of tweed who upbraid their gillies remorselessly in the most forthright terms. But they are best not imitated unless you too are an elderly Duke who dragged said gillie from the falls when they were children together two generations gone, is godfather to his children and pays the wages to boot.

It is remarkable how often fishermen on the opposite bank will disregard even the most basic courtesies. From wading into the middle of the river to better cover your lies, or standing in the middle of a likely pool and broadcasting flies in all directions, to calling noisily to one another upstream and down when I am trying to concentrate. They even cast across you. Who are these people? Where do they come from? Where were they dragged up? I recognise that not everyone has a Granny's knee to learn these principles at, but for Heaven's sake, there are books, aren't there?

It makes me froth and boil, and say short Anglo-Saxon words. In short, rod rage. Oooh! I think I must go and have a lie down.

Guillotining Jelly Babies

I think that I have tried most ways to catch fish. Besides, that is, with a rod and line. I've dabbed about the estuaries and creeks with a trident. I've stalked the banks of rivers and streams with a glaive. I have tickled trout from a hotel brook and I have tried to foul hook a sleeping salmon from a railway bridge. I've lured minnows into a beer bottle with aniseed balls, and I have tried to dynamite carp from the farm pond with crow scarers. All with more or less equal unsuccess.

It is true that I tickled a trout. It is also true that the trout in question was the cook's pet, who enjoyed – apparently – a bit of a tickle as much as anyone, and would lie smiling seraphically on the grassy bank being photographed beside the rod handles of failed fisherfolk who wanted to lie in their holiday snaps and in their teeth, until it was time to be returned to the water with a titbit for his trouble. The aniseed balls were a success too. I was introduced to this form of fishing by my god-daughter. You lie on the bridge over the stream in the garden and dangle a clear glass bottle by a string about its neck in the stream below. When the sticklebacks are enticed within, you hoick it briskly out and decant the captured mites into a bucket. The bottle can be baited according to taste, but for some reason aniseed balls seem favourite.

The carp dynamiting incident was a less than ideal outing of which I am properly ashamed. It was a poorly planned, worse managed and ineptly executed expedition for which we were ill-prepared and wholly under-equipped. No wonder we didn't have any success. The pond was a nasty green and mostly stagnant affair behind the hop drying sheds, but the occasional bubbles and periodic bow waves that broke its scummy surface suggested leviathans below. So we sneaked some crow scarers out of the farm manager's office one evening and with little more ado, lobbed them in the pond. At first they just went out when they hit the water, and then we struck on the wizard wheeze of putting them in a bottle as we lobbed. Now children, don't whatever you do try this at home. For one thing, if those strange fanatical carp men find out about

187

Don't try this at home.

it, they will probably string you up by your heels from the nearest tree and pelt you with boilies and groundbait. And on the other you will probably blow yourselves up. We very nearly did. After several attempts however we did manage to get one to go off underwater. Whereupon a positive cascade of pungent green slime was launched from the surface and was duly dumped on the wee lads cowering on the bank. Of massive carp carcasses we saw nothing. Of the wallpaper in the corner of my father's study for the rest of the weekend, I saw a great deal.

But I think that, in retrospect, the most utterly purposeless fishing expedition I have undertaken must have been the attempt to shoot a pike with a cross-bow. Now one hears of marshland wildfowlers – those great bearded hairy men with waders and colossal guns and the wild staring eyes who can be seen at dusk and dawn striding out into the bundoo beyond the sea wall making ducky noises at one another – one hears of these men returning from wherever it is they go out on the marsh, with sea trout that they have spied cruising up the dyke beside which they are crouched in the mud, and duly shot with their great guns. Which seems reasonable. At least if you think I am going to argue with great bearded hairy men, and heavily armed GBHM at that, about the moral and sporting rights and wrongs of shooting sea trout then you have got another think coming. Anyway back to the pike.

We were camping at the time. Like, in tents. Scout camp, it was, which gives you some idea of how long ago this was. I have grown up a lot since. Well, I have got older anyway. And while we were washing in the stream one morning, we saw the pike. It was not a huge pike; but then again it was not a baby by any means. About eight or ten pounds? Anyway there it lay, under the bank. Just staring at us. As pike will. Well, obviously we went and got rods and lines and we hurled worms and maggots and all sorts past his nose, and he studiously ignored us. As pike will. So we decided to shoot him. We all knew how to make a cross-bow. We used to make them out of our slide rules and a rubber band most days, when we weren't guillotining jelly babies, and shoot each other with pencils. Try making anything interesting out of a calculator; no wonder our schoolchildren are all on drugs; lack of properly healthy activities.

Like shooting one another. So we did the same thing on a grander scale with a couple if stakes and an inner tube, and then attaching the arrow – a bamboo with a nail whipped onto the end (Oh, we were a right creative little bunch. We reckoned there would be badges galore in this for us) - to some binder twine in order to retrieve the quarry, we took ourselves back to the stream. Where the pike waited patiently for us. As pike will.

Alas, for all our design and engineering skills, it was the maths which let us down. We fired into the water with nil effect whatever while the pike merely lurked. Grinning; as pike will. We had encountered the parallax effect. Which means that as the consequence of refracted light molecules accelerating away from one another at a uniformly increasing velocity or something – if I had understood any of this at the time, or even now, then I wouldn't know how to make a cross-bow from a slide-rule, now would I? – the arrow went either over or under the pike which wasn't where it appeared to be but was either above or below where it appeared to be depending on the parallax factor. You see? The parallax effect. QED. And as we argued with one another as to whether we should be shooting above, below or beside the pike, or where the pike appeared to be, in order to allow for the parallax effect, the pike just slipped away. As pike will.

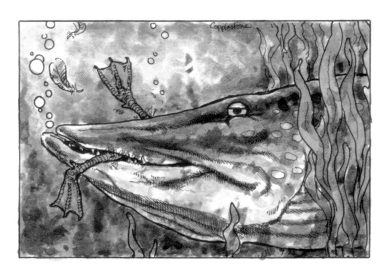

Partridge Palpitations

Who in their right mind would run a syndicate? Who even not in their right mind would run the Boys' Team? These are sound questions and they are particularly apposite when I, for my sins skipper of the said Boys' Team, find myself standing alone in a pub car-park in Oxfordshire on the morning of their first formal outing. "Half past eight sharp in the pub car-park for heart-starter... and please don't be late!" I said in my letter to the Boys setting out the plans for the day and here I am, by myself, at 8.40am, thermos in hand, kicking the tyres and looking at my watch.

It would not perhaps be so bad if we were not going to spend the day on the farm where I shoot regularly during the rest of the season and where they think I am quite scatterbrained enough already. I explained this to the Boys at length when last we met. "Remember, Boys," I instructed them "I have to shoot here later in the year so don't whatever you do let me down." The Boys looked suitably solemn. "We understand," they said. "Best behaviour," they said. "Don't worry," they said. *They said*. So where are they? I shall resign.

Like buses, they all arrive together. Feeble excuses are offered and summarily rejected. Only Neil is forgiven because he has the ticket to prove that he was booked for taking a short cut down a one way street. "I told the constable that I was going partridge shooting," he says appealingly, "but he just didn't care." Really, it undermines one's faith in the Met. It is Neil's considered view that in any civilised society such an explanation would have resulted in a couple of motorcycle outriders, complete with sirens and flashing lights, being summoned to ease him through the rush hour traffic. Instead he has the summons. Well, there you go. Just wait till I'm in charge, then you'll see changes.

Introductions for the day's guests all round and we push off towards the farm in line astern. Good little ducks all in a row. One disadvantage of meeting up away from the final venue is that our kind host, who was expecting us several minutes ago, is looking round the empty farmyard at the allotted time and at the groups of beaters standing about waiting for the fun to begin, wondering if he's got the right day. His relief is palpable when the Boys arrive like a cavalry chargette at a collected canter. The final piece of the jig-saw falls into place. Birds, blue sky, beaters, Guns. That is the natural order of things.

By now my first worry has been replaced by the second concern of the Captain's day. Will there be anything for the Boys to shoot? After all, I choose the venues; I do the contracts; I take hefty slices of the Boys' hard-earned during the course of the year and they have expectations. While the Boys boot and spur themselves I have a quiet word with our host.

"No worries on that score," says he, cheerfully, "there are partridges everywhere. We had a flawless rearing programme and the weather has been fantastic. I've never seen so many partridges." Super. Wonderful. If he's that confident the place must be ankle deep in the little blighters. Worry number two is now replaced by worry number three. The Boys will go mad and shoot the lot.

We are on the standard deal for this kind of expedition. Likely bag X; a few either side and never a word said. Over the odds by a

The Captain's nightmare.

country mile and it's out with the wallet. I am trying wherever possible these days to veer away from hard and fast number crunching and the skilful shoot manager is becoming a craftsman at managing the day to achieve the sort of (actually rather modest) bags that are the Boys' Team objectives. However this is the first day out and trigger fingers will be itching. So a word is in order. I call the team to order.

"Boys," I say in headmasterly tone, "The Boss informs me that there are great numbers of partridges on the ground. The weather is fine and conditions good. We shall doubtless see a fine show of birds, so please, please, please...be discreet." I also tell them to be safe, safe, safe. They are all experienced and of sound mind and I would take them anywhere; but you can't say it too often.

We draw for pegs, mount up and ride to the first drive. The sun is breaking through and the dew is twinkling on the rape. The Sherpa (bless her) suggests that I should stop worrying. It's easy for her to say.

The first drive is off the brow of the hill. The farm is usefully set out in this respect having what amounts to a large bowl in the centre. Some shrewd planting by our host's forbears of spinneys on the top of the bowl at the principal points of the compass, and the equally shrewd planting by our host of game cover "tails" behind these spinneys, means that the Guns can be planted in the foot of the depression and face two or possibly three drives from almost the same position by moving to face the different coppices, depending on the wind direction. While the beaters blank into the first spinney, the Boys line out, and worry number four surfaces. Will the Boys be able to hit anything?

A solitary pigeon floats out of the spinney, dislodged by the approaching beaters. It wafts towards the line of waiting Guns. As it approaches I can see a couple of the Boys practising their swings. The pigeon drifts over the middle of the line. Nothing happens. The pigeon flies on unmolested. The Boys are clearly taking no chances.

Our host, who is standing just behind me, looks puzzled. "Best behaviour," I offer in explanation. "Should I give them a whistle?" he asks. "Better had," I agree. He gives a long blast on his whistle and the Boys break out into more swinging; there are a series of clicks and clunks as guns are readied for action. I breathe a sigh of relief in the realisation that we have narrowly avoided a shotless drive as the result of the Boys putting behaviour before barrage and refusing to fire before the whistle. Now we are ready.

The first covey breaks out of the spinney. They head towards the centre of the line. We watch. I desperately want to see some birds taken; but not too many. Coco the dog wants to see everything on the deck so that she can show off in the pick up. Our host wants to get the day off to a successful start. Only the Sherpa is calm, watching the covey flare over the line with a discerning eye. A crackle of shots echo round the bowl and two or three birds bundle down. One staggers and continues past the line. A single shot and it falls abruptly in front of one of the pickers-up. "That will be Angus tidying up," says the Sherpa approvingly. "Well done," says our host. "Phew," says I.

The coveys begin to emerge at intervals now. Some swinging to the right or left, some over the middle of the line. A lone pair come straight over my peg and I kill the higher of the two cleanly with the first barrel showing a masterly discernment and diplomacy. Our host murmurs "Good shot", Coco sits up to mark the fallen bird and the Sherpa smiles. Up and down the line there are sporadic shots and birds tumble hither and yon. Everyone appears to have a shot and at the end of the drive the Boys forgather with many "Oohs" and "Aahs" and "Did you see the one that'ses".

Now I can relax. Or at least begin to do so. We have a bag, or the beginnings of one. Some of the Boys have hit some of the partridges so they will be happy. Well, the Boys will be; the partridges may have another view. Miffed, I shouldn't wonder, or would rather have been. Our host has said something approving; and all the Guns and beaters have survived the first onslaught. The sun is still shining and all is going swimmingly.

After the second drive we have a bit of a break for sip of something modest. This is partially to give the beaters time to regroup and do some blanking in and partially to slow down the Boys who have been showing a very satisfactory restraint but have nontheless been belting partridges both long and tall for six in a notable reversal of their form at the shooting school a few weeks earlier where we assembled for a bit of a pre-season loosener and where they resolutely missed everything but the proving plate.

As I tidy the glasses back into the boot of the car and move to my peg for the third drive I can see the Boys all huddled together round one peg arguing over who is which number, and who is certain he was this before, because he was between you two wasn't he? or not? weren't you? They end up two to a peg facing the wrong direction before I intervene.

I ask you? Who in their right mind?

Will the Boys be able to hit anything?

Reservoir Dogs

Let's consider, for a moment, big reservoirs. There are good features and bad about big lakes. The good features tend to be that you are allowed to use a motor, whereas on smaller lakes, meres and ponds, you are generally speaking required to do the old slave galley thing and take a turn at the oars. Which is fine if you used to row for Oxford, or if you are a bit of a fitness freak, or if you like rowing. It is even alright if it is a bright, clear, sunny and happy morning and the row out to the likely spots is filled with the joys of Spring, thoughts of a day with the fish and a brisk and warming twenty minutes of in and out. It's a different question though when you are toiling back from the far end of the reservoir, it's raining, again, as it has been all bloody day. It's been getting progressively chillier since sunset. There's a nasty chop now developing in the rising head-wind that sends a fine spray over the bows, and down your neck – as if it mattered by now – every fourth stroke. You have been deep fishing a sinking line all day. And needless to add, you haven't had a sniff. The coffee's cold; the whisky's finished; and there's the sting of a blister forming in between the thumb and forefinger of one hand. Only finding yourself locked out of the car when you get back can add to the sum of misery which is a reservoir then.

The motor they let one use on the big waters however may get you home faster; but because of the corresponding size of the place, it won't get you home any sooner. So you can sit huddled in the back in the rain for quite as long while you are putt-putting home, as you do paddling. At least paddling gives you something to do.

As does catching a trolling line, or even just a trailing line, round the propeller as you go. The time from the first moment of fierce delight as the reel squeals, to the dawning horror and frantic switching off of things as the tip of the rod arches dangerously over the end of the dinghy is but a few seconds. There are those who might well point out that it's worth it for that split second when you think it might be a fish. These are sad people. These are people who don't open letters from

198

There's a nasty chop developing.

the Reader's Digest because they like to fantasise for a while about the millions they might have won. Let me tell you, trying to disentangle the remains of 60 metres of a once-decent forward taper from the blade of an outboard in rising wind and failing light, can be no-one's idea of a price worth paying.

Now it is the rising wind which brings me to my next point. Not that I suffer from it, myself, but that's another story altogether. The effect that the breeze tends to have though, particularly those of us who are partial to a tinny or three while we are having a bit of a float and a fish, is to put a bit of pressure on the bladder. Now these days when this happens, I don't have a problem – at least not as long as I am at the leeward end of the boat that is, and if you are not sure why that should be important, I suggest you go and ask a sailor. If you know a sailor.

It is just a case of up and out, as the saying goes, and over the side. That after all is what the picnic pipe is for. But when I was but a wee – if that is not the wrong expression – slip of a lad, one did not feel entirely comfortable standing in the front of the boat foaming up the downwind side. Well, you don't. What with the other chaps there and everything. Now I realise that my problems then were as nothing compared to what is to come when the mechanics pack up completely and the whistling wind forces me to the bow end every five minutes only to find that the self same breeze renders it impossible to do anything constructive once there.

There is a situation which is a hundred times worse, a thousand times. When the torture is doubled and re-doubled by the mere sight of land in the distance and the rumbling certainty that if it were only a few yards away it would still be too far. I know. I've been there. Let's not explore it.

So what are the virtues of reservoirs? Well, for one thing we can be sure that there are some fish in them. The management count them in and the management count them out again; and cormorants notwithstanding, the ones which are left should be big ones. Now here is not the time or place to get into the small and lively large and log-like debate. And I defy anyone not to enjoy having caught a seriously big fish. And that being the case, reservoirs are the places to do it.

So every now and again I like to be a reservoir dog, though these days I tend to stay close enough to the side to get out now and again when the need arises.

Last Cast

Every now and again in life you are fortunate enough to meet someone who is a real expert. If, like me, you are something of an enthusiastic amateur who slides by on a modicum of knowledge, occasional bursts of unaccountable skill, a good deal of holding forth in a forthright and determined way designed to muddy waters, blur definitions and generally cover up for an almost complete lack of any real understanding of what you are talking about and once in a blue moon, outrageous flukes, then these periodic encounters with true expertise can be somewhat unsettling.

In fact, my first school report contained a comment from an acutely perceptive form master who wrote "Giles must realise that a superficial knowledge of his subject supported by glib conversation and a winning smile is no substitute for real understanding. There are two ways to find it out. This is the easy one." You can't get much past a good teacher, can you?

I have been found out a fair number of times since, with more or less embarrassment and I have indeed learned that a solid understanding of the subject really will get you further in the long run. In the shorter term however, I am still of the view that fast talking and wild leaps of faith may yet keep your head above water long enough to reach the door before the furniture starts flying.

However, I have also learned that when you do meet a real expert, and assuming that you have not already made a complete arse of yourself in open court on their specialist subject, the thing to do is to plant yourself at their feet and learn as much as possible before they either trip over you or hurl you bodily from the portals.

Assuming, that is, that they are an agreeable sort of person. Experts do fall, it seems to me, into two distinct camps. On the one hand there are pompous drones who correct you on every tiny point, blind you with their dazzling breadth of knowledge and who bore for Britain on their subject of choice. Then there are those who share their expertise

...*who bore for Britain on their subject of choice.*

without lecturing, strew your train of thought with little clues such that you end up working things out for yourself and lavish praise upon your bungling efforts while disparaging their own massive achievements as being largely luck. On reflection, I suppose that the former just know a lot of stuff and the latter are natural teachers. And there is all the difference in the world between the two.

When I was much younger the Aging Progenitor used to take me fishing at Grafham. I didn't enjoy it much, to be honest. Not least because he always invited along the same truly obnoxious expert. He was a friend, I suppose, and he certainly had all the gear and was forever taking temperatures and catching flies in his butterfly net and changing lures and pouring out torrents of advice. No, it wasn't advice – that's the point – it was criticism. "Don't do it like that." "You don't want one of those on." "You're not still using that, are you?" All the time. He killed a lot of fish, to be sure. He'd have his limit by the time the rest of us had caught anything, and then he'd start on ours. He was an expert, to be sure; he was also a know-all. It's a fine line, but fatal.

The other day, *au contraire*, I had the privilege to fish with a genuine, dyed in the wool, fully paid-up expert. Fortunately I was forewarned so I didn't ask him, for example, if he wanted me to tie his flies on for him. Or point out that his leader was way too short. Or that I thought a Cat's Whisker with a tad of weight should just about hit the spot this morning. Actually he did ask me what I thought might work, which of course pleased me immensely. So immensely that I ignored the fact that he promptly did the opposite. But that's the skill, isn't it? He didn't ram his opinion down my throat: he simply followed his own furrow and got on with catching fish. The rest of us, natch, copied him the moment we decently could.

Every now and again he wondered out loud "if we might have a bit of luck with….?" this or that combination. Or asked "Isn't it the case that in circumstances like this we should try…?" so and so. Or "Does anyone think we should doing….?" some such. Immediately following each of these quiet proposals, we were all feverishly ferreting in our bags and baskets for anything which remotely resembled whatever he was talking about. If he said he'd heard somewhere that a bit of tin foil and a bent pin was as good as anything, you can bet we'd all have been giving it a lash by lunchtime. And a good deal of the time he just spent sitting about chatting. It seemed at the time that he couldn't get enough of our conversation and was genuinely interested in our opinions on everything from the best tube for spring fishing in Iceland to "The Euro: Yes or No?" I suspect in retrospect it was merely his means of stretching his limit of ludicrously easy trout into something more than a short morning.

It was, I will freely admit, an unalloyed pleasure. And I learned a good deal into the bargain. Which means that I stand just a hair's breadth more chance of getting away with it the next time I bump into someone who really knows what they are talking about.

And I might catch more fish.

Sixteen Bores

First up I shoot with 16 bores. From time to time I am asked why? There are in fact two answers; one is slightly longer than the other. The short version is that beggars can't be choosers, and when I had finally scrimped and saved enough of the necessary to buy a decent gun, I was not exactly faced with a free choice. To which you might reasonably respond "Save up some more," but I am very much afraid that is beyond me. Once I have any sort of a wedge, it is destined for the till.

So when I see what is by all accounts a deeply agreeable English sidelock advertised at an even more deeply agreeable price, then I am inclined to overlook the fact that it is a 16 bore and focus only on the essentials; which are, in no particular order, that it is seriously cute; and I can afford it.

The longer answer takes us back to the days when I was first allowed out with a keeper friend, to follow him on his round, to lug barrels of water about the estate, to heft sacks of grain into the pens and to shift the bantam coops onto fresh grass. All of which effort was rewarded by being lent Harry's folding .410 and a handful of Fourlongs and spending a hour at dusk patrolling the meadows and hedges behind the cottage in pursuit of rabbits or the odd pigeon. Indeed it would have to be a very odd pigeon indeed to get knocked over by a kid with a tiny gun like that. I know that there are great Shots who swear by their early training, potting pigeons with a popgun, and even greater Shots who insist that they can do it still. But I would challenge any of them to knock down a pigeon on the wing with a .410, without stuffing the first two-thirds of its tiny barrel with some Double Magnum Total Nutter No.7 cartridge, which has an impact like an artillery barrage and a recoil like a Howitzer.

The standard team of .410, Fourlong and a kid produces a curious hunched figure, inclined to creep ever so slowly towards hedge corners,

Sweet sixteens.

and then spring gazelle-like into the open poised for action. Or as poised as you can be for action when you have still to claw back the corroded hammer, as bunnies hop and lollop in all directions.

Naturally therefore as soon as I had washed enough windows, mown enough lawns and diligently invested the occasional Postal Orders from sundry Godparents and the like, I blew the lot on a 20 bore. You do, don't you? Well, you shouldn't. And more particularly, you should not then progress to a 12 bore. For the record, yes I did that too.

Instead, the way to go is out of step with the rest of the world. Now this may just be me trying to be non-conformist and rebellious. Easy-rider, man! That's me. But on the other hand there may very well be some sense in all of this. If you finish with the 16 bore, this means that the logical starting place is the 28 bore. Now I just happen to have one of these as well. It is a perfectly charming little piece that I bought a few years ago, allegedly in preparation for the future training of sundry children that I don't yet have. In the meantime however it has been brought out from time to time for various girlfriends to have a bang with at clays and the like. It is, as a matter of fact, terrific fun to take the little gun and a couple of boxes of shell to a shooting ground and to have a belt at the clays oneself. You have to do more of everything with the smaller bore. More swing, more lead, more accuracy. It is quite a learning experience I can tell you.

Having said which, the tinies can get on with it too. You can knock down a decent clay bird with it, and you can powder, when you concentrate, the simple incoming target, more times than not. And that is what young beginners really need. Lots of results, lots of the time. Four-tenning away is so-oo-oo-o dull. I think it was probably a year before I actually managed to creep close enough to something to actually belt it in the ear successfully. It is true that no benighted pigeon has ever been borne home in quite such triumph but it is also true that I came within a gnat's whatsit of packing the whole thing in before that bird chose foolishly to roost in that particular tree.

Anyway the upshot is simple: better by far to begin with something which is even moderately effective, than something which merely goes bang. In addition to which, the speedy progression between 28 to 16 means that the overall budget only has to stretch to two guns rather than three, and that means more shells for both. However, there is one drawback. You know how a 20 bore cartridge will slip into the breech of a 12 bore just far enough to have a 12 gauge fall in behind it? Well, the same is true of a 28 gauge shell going into a 16 bore breech.

So mind how you go.

Small Bags, Big Fun

I like autumn. Spring is fun; but governed almost entirely by hormones and not to be relied upon. I'm no anthropologist but it always seems to me that folk in Spring are about as dependable as bears just emerging from a long hibernation. They tend to be a bit dopey and interested in little more than food and a decent gargle and are amenable to being stroked a bit, and then suddenly, for no apparent reason, they go all grizzly on you and start growling something fearsome. Of course, I'm no different and can react quite strangely to being stroked. It rather depends on who is doing the stroking, as a matter of fact.

Summer is a long hot lounge on the beach. Lots of food. Long lunches on the terrace which are all of a sudden dinner. Picnics in the sunshine with a decent Chablis and a deal of recreational stroking. Warm evenings with moths fluttering about the candles and starry skies above. There's a great deal to be said for summer, now you come to think

209

about it.

Autumn however brings shooting, and with it a fever that never palls. For those who squeeze in a solid three weeks at the grouse, a dozen stags and several days at the partridges in October, I dare say that the tingle has already been and gone, but for the rest of us this is where we start contemplating a nicely filling diary, ordering cartridges and generally getting the kit together for the excitements ahead.

I wonder if it's just me, or do I detect that there is a change drifting through our sport like the tang of a bonfire on an autumn breeze? Looking at the dates in the diary, there are invitations hither and yon. Still plenty of spaces if anyone is interested though. The days which are highlighted, the red star outings, are not the biggest or the smartest however. They are all mates days. They are all jollies with shooting attached rather than the other way round.

There are no promises of great quantities of game. In fact this one promises little more than an armed walk and then lunch. I doubt if there will even be what can be described as a drive. We shall walk in one direction and then mooch back in another. The chances are that we shall stumble over a pheasant or two and I know that there is a pond which can be relied upon to have a brace of mallard floating about on it, but they are usually seen departing at high speed from the opposite side of the copse to the one we are approaching. They usually hear us coming.

And there's no surprise to that because we are usually quite an animated little group. Quite apart from the gaggle of wholly unsuitable dogs who are running riot about the place, and the recent recruitment of several offspring who insist they want to join the fun at breakfast and who by midmorning are whingeing about being cold or damp or hungry or tired or missing their Gameboy, we always seem to be laughing at something. And the mallard hear us coming and depart from the other edge of the copse and then we have a laugh about that, and there is much commentary about how the duck must be able to set their calendars by their annual trip to pastures new and then we walk back up the beat for elevens. The whole day's huge fun, and yet I doubt that we end up with enough for a bird a head.

Or here's another annual invitation. It's a farm shoot way out in the Fen. It's not an unserious affair actually. There are beaters and proper dogs and there are drives and whistles. There are even very occasional pheasants who do as Fen pheasants are wont to do; which is to take off vertically at the instant the first beater puts a foot into the cover to a point where it is almost indistinguishable from the leaden sky behind it, and then zoom straight towards the biggest gap in the line which, if you are lucky, is you. There are always lots of Guns and the chances of a pheasant choosing you is remote, but when one does, you run the full gamut of emotions from fear and frenzy to fury and frustration and occasional elation in a few seconds flat. And if you hit one, all the Guns cheer like anything, and if you miss, the beaters all boo. It's a strange affair alright; but it's great fun.

And there's the key, isn't it? It's great fun. I enjoy standing in a line of seasoned Guns confronting a steady flow of pheasants. In fact, I absolutely love it. I think that participating in a classic pheasant drive, delivered by a keeper who really knows his stuff, in a team who really know how to shoot is a rare and special thing. But I also think that sitting on a bale chewing a hot sausage butty and juggling a tin mug of modest claret and looking at the three cocks and a rabbit which make up the entire bag for the morning, and having a laugh about it with a few mates, is terribly, terribly important.

Maybe I'm just getting old.

First Catch Your Halibut

Everyone seems to be talking about fishing in Alaska these days. Land of the 20lb steelhead and the 70lb king salmon; of sockeyes and chinooks. As well they might be; for make no mistake, the fish are there in prodigious quantities and tremendous sport can be had in breathtaking countryside for the price of a week flogging a short stretch of a Scottish river to a salmon-free foam. I know. I've been to Alaska. Before it was fashionable naturally.

What they don't tell you is that Alaska is still a wild place, not merely in terms of the rugged countryside but the fairly rugged nature of the folk who inhabit it. There is a saying that when the Pilgrim Fathers landed in the New World the whole place tilted; and all the rolling stones ended up in California – where they invented cinema, founded Hollywood, learned how to surf and discovered rock and roll. Oh, and found a lot of gold, of course. Meanwhile, however, all the loose screws ended up in Alaska, where they have done precious little ever since. They are all charming as all get-out, but when ambitions were being distributed the Alaskans had popped outside for a smoke.

I recall one evening which may give you a whiff of what I'm talking about: We were sitting on the porch of a lodge several miles from the next habitation on the edge of the sound, which is like a big fiord, drinking beer and wondering what to do about supper when we saw Sam's boat roaring across the water.

He was going full throttle by the sound of it and showed no signs of slowing down. Indeed we wondered if all was well with him as he headed straight for the beach in front of us with no sign whatever of the engine slackening for an instant. And we were positively startled when, instead of cutting his engines and gliding gracefully to the pontoon like a normal person, Sam proceeded to ram his pride and joy straight up the shingle where it gently keeled over into the goose-tongue grass and Sam fell out of the cockpit and onto the beach.

"What-ho!" he said cheerily. This was largely for my benefit. I

"I took to the beast with a baseball bat."

had explained to Sam in the bar some nights previously that all English people spoke as if stepping directly from the pages of a PG Wodehouse novel.

"What-ho yourself," said Gail, my hostess, "and what are you doing ramming my beach this fine evening, if I may ask?"

Sam looked properly embarrassed. "Sinking, actually," he said. "I only just made it this far. Boat's full of water." And why was Sam sinking? Halibut. Fishing for halibut is both sport and recreation in this part of the world and Sam is one of that resolute breed who persist in long-lining for the great triangular flatfish.

This involves trailing dozens of lines several fathoms deep from the transom and trolling them over likely halibut lies and tugging at them now and again to see if a halibut has taken a lure deep in the water below. Once a halibut is hooked all the other lines are brought in and the lucky bait – and the unlucky halibut are then dragged hand over hand to the surface.

It's pretty Stone Age stuff, to be honest and there are more sophisticated and commercial ways to do it, but like I said, they're really not that concerned in Alaska. Anyoldhow, this halibut was not inclined to come quietly. It was not, said Sam, an especially big fish, less than 200lbs, but kinda frisky, if you know what I mean. He got it to the surface after half an hour's toil but as the fish broke the surface and saw what was going on it went berserk and set off for the bottom once again; taking most of the skin off Sam's palms with it for good measure.

The second time he got the fish up to the top, Sam got a shark hook into him with a buoy attached before it set off for the bottom once more and Sam would have cut the line and let the buoy bring the fish up in due season. The tide was against him though and he would lose fish and gear if he left them out there overnight.

So he set about hauling the great fish up again. "The third time I got that bastard on the top," said Sam " I took at him with a baseball bat. But all he does is break my damn nose with his tail and heads down again." By this time, according to Sam, Sam's general good humour was wearing what can only be described as thin. Again he brought the fish, fighting foot by foot, to the surface. And this time he was standing for no more nonsense. With his feet braced against the thwart, he got his gaff firmly in the halibut's gills and hoicked the damn fish over the gunwale and dumped him onto the deck at last.

And then for good measure he hauled out his pistol "and shot that bastard fish half a dozen times in his damn fool head!" And since it was quite a big pistol, he also put half a dozen holes through the bottom of his boat in the process. Hence the emergency docking procedure.

We offered Sam our commiserations and a beer. And we promised to help him mend his boat in the morning. And we invited him to stay the night and to join us for supper. We had, we explained, been on the cusp of deciding what to eat.

I can confirm to you that fresh barbecued halibut, albeit fairly peppered, is a meal for princes.

That's Alaskan fishing for you.

Creature from the Black Lagoon

There is a sequel to the story of Sam and the halibut. It is not by way of being an especially edifying tale and yet it characterises once more the thoroughly pragmatic approach folk adopt towards life in the Alaskan woods and waterways and the extraordinary diversity of the wildlife which is quite literally within reach.

My friend Denny and his pal Tom were upriver, notionally checking their crab-pots, but also reconnoitring the streams for the start of the silver salmon runs that would bring hordes of free-spending fishermen north for the annual salmon derby. It's an odd thought, isn't it, that while a salmon fisherman in Britain will count himself many times blessed on any day that he actually makes contact with a fish, in Alaska they actually have competitions which are won, not by the angler with the biggest fish, nor yet by the competitor with the most fish, nor even the fisherman with the greatest weight of fish – any one of which can be achieved with an early start and a modicum of hard work. No, the big prize goes to the bloke who lands the silver salmon with the gold tag on it. Now, that's a lottery.

Whatever, Tom and Denny are mooching about upriver when they see a pink blob lying on the marsh. They amble over expecting some piece of flotsam. A length of net from a passing trawler perhaps, or a boat-cover washed up by the tide. What they discovered, *au contraire*, was the mortal remains of a giant squid – 15 foot long from the tip of its great cape to the end of its tentacles. Presumably it had been pursuing some shoal or other of potential prey up the sound and had become stranded. It was either a smallish giant squid, or a hell of a big ordinary one.

So they took a few photographs of it. And they took photographs of each other with it. And they videoed each other stalking the sea monster. "You only have the chance for one shot with these bigguns! Har. Har. Har." "The key with yer big squid is to get between it and the water, see? Har. Har. Har." And so on and so forth. Then they wondered

…one deceased tentacle around Sam's ankle.

what to do next. They settled on a plan and began to drag the squid across the marsh towards the skiff.

The upshot was that, as dusk fell that evening, Denny and Tom burst into the bar back in the village, ashen faced and gabbling that they had just narrowly escaped a gruesome death when their skiff had been attacked by a giant squid as they had returned from their crabbing expedition. The assembled company stared politely into their beer as the guys blathered on about the monster pursuing them through the twilight.

Then Tom looks through the window to the dock below and reels back in alarm. "God help us!" he squeaks, "It's coming up the dock!" And with a scream for effect that would have done credit to a pantomime dame, he staggers back towards the bar.

Now it happened that Sam the halibut shooter had been on a fishing trip for several days. Accordingly he had started drinking somewhat earlier than most of the others in the room and was perhaps, as the consequence, not thinking altogether as clearly as he might. Moving, glass in hand, towards the window he glances – ever so casually – down towards the pontoon. And there in the half-light, he sees the artfully arranged carcass of the giant squid apparently in the act of dragging itself out of the water onto the boardwalk.

To do the man justice, what followed was an act of very considerable bravery when all is said and done, because it was indeed the act of a courageous man to yank the door open and to stagger off down the path to confront the monster hand to tentacle. Of course, being Sam, he had his pistol and he was not slow to demonstrate that he knew how to use it. It seemed, however, to have a somewhat limited effect. With every round he let off, the kraken at the edge of the dock simply shuddered and stayed put. So with his ammunition quickly expended, Sam launched himself at the monster. Or more particularly he launched one wellied foot at the creature's ghastly, glassy, staring eye.

Unfortunately the squid responded by wrapping one deceased tentacle around Sam's ankle and then proceeded to slide gently off into the water dragging the unhappy fisherman with it. Contrary to the normal course of events when man and cephalopod collide, especially in the water which is, after all, pretty much cephalopod home turf, Sam promptly sank like a stone while the squid bobbed about on the surface in a rather gassy and bloated way. As Sam eventually surfaced, spluttering, once more it was the work of a moment for someone to grab him by the collar and hoick him onto the deck. Meanwhile the squid continued to bob gently about a few feet away.

It is, I'm told, still a question of heated debate at what point the harsh realities of the situation dawned on soggy Sam. Some say that he saw the light the moment that his head broke the surface. Others assert that they saw the light in his eyes as he stood dripping on the deck and the first giggles started. There are those who state categorically that he still didn't get it until Tom and Denny started haring back towards the bar howling with mirth. What all are agreed upon however is that it was a damn good job that Sam had used up all his bullets on the squid because it would have been touch and go whether the boys would have made it up the boardwalk otherwise. It took a goodly while and a great deal of beer before communications, let alone cordiality, were finally restored between the parties.

Then again it is a hard thing for fellow fishermen to hold grudges. Especially in a small community. In Alaska. When the silver salmon are running.

A Feel for Eels

Now I dare say that by now you lot believe that I have lost the plot completely. Pike last month and now eels. Eels, of all things. Nasty, slimy evil looking things. Ugh! Foo yuk ping!

And, happen, you'd be right. But I got to thinking about eels and before I long I was well lost in a world of fish a fair mile from these hallowed pages.

First up, your common or garden eel – *Anguilla anguilla* to us eggheads – is very like your far from common or garden salmon. It migrates. But here is where the story tends to get a bit wobbly, because while it is the case that we have examined all aspects of the lifestyle of the noble salmon in order, quite properly, better to conserve and enhance its environs and – quite coincidentally – our own chances of catching one, about the humble eel we know almost nothing.

Bare facts:- elvers come upstream in the spring. They are so tiny that they are almost see-through, no bigger than a pin, and they are caught by their tens of thousands in hand nets. Some are fried or omeletted right there on the riverbank, such is the delicacy and rarity of the dish, while others are saved for stocking elsewhere. The Europeans, needless to say, having eaten theirs to oblivion already. Huge numbers are exported, notably to Asia.

Those that get by the netsmen plough upstream and then they vanish. Oh, anglers come across them from time to time, either by accident or design, but the vast majotiy of these survivors disperse themselves about the place in muddy tributaries and lurk about the place for the foreseeable future, bottom feeding and waxing fat. And quite fat they can get too. It is recorded that when they drained the Whittlesey Mere some blokes came across a very fat eel indeed. So fat that they stuck a pitchfork between its eyes. Not that it noticed much; with a wriggle it snapped the haft and then, pausing only to break one of the men's legs, it slithered up over the bank and into the river and away.

And then one day they head back to the sea. No one knows

"Then yew heng 'im up by the match…"

when exactly or why. They just do. Full moon? Midsummer's Eve? Water warmer than air? Who knows? Your guess is as good as anyone's. They don't all go together necessarily, generation by generation. As far as anyone knows they don't go in alphabetical order or by seniority. Or at least they might; we simply don't know. What we do know is that they will leave no stone unturned to get there. My friend Jack, who lives out on the Broads, recounts how he was coming back from the pub, quite late, and a heavy dew was laid on the meadow as he ambled towards his cottage when the ground came alive with eels of all sizes, in their hundreds, wriggling their way from ponds and streams and dykes back to the mother Broad and thence to the sea. "Swimmin' threw th' damp they was," he say to me. "Swimming threw th' dew. An' tha's upwards of a mile, yew know."

And once back into the sea they swim all the way to the Sargasso Sea – we think – and there in the great floating kelp beds they breed – though no one has ever actually confirmed the fact. And then they die. Or perhaps they don't. Because there have been some very big eels found, or reported to have been found, or perhaps rumoured to have been found – it's a bit of a slippery area – and it is feasible, they say, that the female of the species, at least, could live as long as twenty years or more. Perhaps. Though they are not sure about that, obviously. Which suggests that some at least do come back from the Sargasso after spawning, or from wherever it is that they go to spawn if that is what they go to do. Or maybe some of them, or some of the females at least, don't go anywhere at all but just stay where they were and get bigger. Or go later. We just don't know, you see. Eels not being very glamorous or attractive, no one has taken much of an interest in them, to be honest. It is all about as clear as mud.

Anyoldhow, the babies then float back across the Atlantic on the Gulf Stream. Or not, as the case may be, since no one has ever caught one. Although, there again, no one has ever really been looking for them. And then they come upstream as shoals of little elvers.
But if one night as you stagger, nay stroll, back from the pub or as it might be the parish council meeting, across the dew-laden grass o'er

the lea and should you happen to see the ground writhing with a mass of eels, remember this! The way to kill an eel is to grab it firmly by the head and crack it like a whip. No, not the head, the tail. Crack it by the tail and its brains fly out between its teeth. Or should you whack it on the head? Or was that the tail? Either way it makes no odds. Head or tail, and there are those who will vigorously endorse either end, and bugger all eventuates.

Jack told me how to do it. "Dew yew grab im firm, boy," says he "an' jam a match between 'is jaws. Iffen 'e dun't fit, ole eel 'ent big enuff, 'n dew yew drop 'im back. Then yew heng 'im by the match on a branch 'n drown the bugger in air. 'S only way." Which is no more unlikely as any of the other ways I have heard suggested and demonstrates exactly the depth of research that has been applied to the whole area. And then you can skin him and jelly him or stew him and delicious indeed he'll be. And keep that skin for boots. All the old Broadsmen used to wear eel-skin boots. Or sword handles. I know that we don't use swords to anything near the extent that we used to, but an eel-skin hilt was the last word in decent sabre circles. Today you could use it on the handlebars of your bicycle, perhaps, or something else you wanted to get a firm grip on. A harpoon say; or a lover.

If you take my advice though, you'll hot smoke him. Then skin and fillet him – which is the work of a moment, I promise you – and pop about an inch at a time on some hot toast with a dab of creamed horse-radish underneath him. Fantastico! And that, if I'm completely honest, is all I really know about eels.

New Gear

I've bought some new gear. In fact it's fair to say I have bought all new gear. The works. And a motorbike to go with it. No. That's not really fair. I bought the motorbike first. I was sitting in the car, sweltering, with the sun beating down and the temperature steadily rising. Watching the little gauge thingy on the dashboard as it crept remorselessly towards the red line. I knew what would happen when it got there. I had passed several unhappy motorists along the way to whom it had already happened. The engine explodes. And it ruins your day; if not your week. The dial in my brain was edging very much the same way. Towards lift-off. There's nothing to be done, of course, you just have to maintain a stoical Zen-like calm until it's over.

Unless you are on a motorbike, of course. There seemed to be an endless procession of these sliding down between the lanes of stationary traffic. Oh, sure, lanes. We're on a motorway, naturally, designed to ease congestion, reduce journey times and generally enrich the motoring experience. Hah!! In your dreams. It really got on my wick I can tell you. By the time I got to the pond, the rise was over and all the local fishers were tidying their tackle away for the brief journey home, and logging their limits in the book in the hut. They wished me well; but I could see from their looks that they were pitying me my forlorn several hours of fishless flogging to come before the long slow journey home. If I wanted to make it back home before midnight, I would have to leave before the evening rise, into the bargain. It made me want to spit. Or more especially it made me want a motorbike. So when I did eventually get home I put one on the shopping list.

To be completely honest several months went by before I got round to it, there being such inconvenient little details as having to get a licence. And learn how to ride. And passing a test. And suchlike hurdles. But tish and pish, these are but flea-bites on the rhino hide of Life, and were quickly resolved. And the upshot was that I got myself a bike. To be exact I got myself a rorty-torty, black as bedamned, nose on the petrol tank and bum in air sportster, which is frightening to behold and completely sphincter threatening to ride. And a hat, sorry, helmet; to go with it.

However when the moment came to take the brute fishing, a slight bug appeared in the ointment. I looked at the bike and I looked at the gear. Now, I have mentioned before the elderliness of the equipment. Or if I haven't I should have. My father, whose accumulation of tackle this largely is, or was until recently, was a discriminating, if eclectic buyer of fishing gear. Accordingly we have a couple of nice rods by Hardy, with reels to match. Greenharts, a Bob Church, floating lines, sinkers, sink tips and more fly boxes than you could shake a stick at. He is less discriminating in his abuse of his belongings. The rods do now live in cases. Acquired somewhat after the event, following the car-boot incident, over which we shall draw a discreet veil, except to recall that it involved six inches out of the middle, the middle mark you, of the best rods.

The reels have been variously dropped in fresh and sea water in their time and have collected enough sand and gravel in their inner workings to open a small, but thriving, aggregates business. The kit lives in the creel. A wicker basket of such antiquity that it is uncertain how much of it is wicker these days and how much is string, nylon and Araldite holding the remains together. And the landing net is a very snappy bamboo affair, much bound with brass, and not designed to be folded into anything less than a family sized shooting brake. Without the family.

Now strapping this lot on the bike was never going to be an option. Quite apart from the fact that I would end up looking like Sir Lancelot, with a good deal of rod sticking out fore, and probably aft, the creel would never make it past 30 mph, and if it did most of the contents would be spread somewhere on the tarmac anyway. The idea of zooming through the traffic trailing several hundred yards of assorted sinkers and shooting heads while distributing lures hither and yon to the four winds was not appealing. And since neither the kit nor the bike could be adapted - something would have to be changed.

The creel would never make it past 30 mph.

Which is how I came to be casting a pretty decent line down Sackville Street, off Piccadilly the other day. Sackville Street is the home of Orvis whose gear I have long admired from trips to the US. Very functional, very efficient. Very American. And what I was after was efficiency. They did look at me a bit blankly when I said I required a motorbike trout rod. I suspect they had some picture of very high speed trolling for an instant. But the fog cleared after I pointed out the machine in question outside their window, and soon I was gripping a deeply agreeable 10 foot graphite four piece, which could be stowed and transported in safety in a stainless steel tube strapped along the saddle. A neatly folded net would lie along side it. For the sake of completeness I added a Battenkill reel and a new floating line. Because I am hopeless in fishing shops I also bought a really neat fly-box, and as a consequence, of course, a handful - well, box full - of flies to go with it.

The point is that I am now completely togged up with new gear. It must be admitted that I get some strange looks when I'm fishing in the very natty electric-blue, skin-tight, one piece leathers, but then into every life a little rain must fall. And I am never entirely happy when carrying home the day's bag. The idea of broadcasting trout at high speed through the traffic is too gruesome to contemplate.

On the other hand, sometimes as I'm winding through the traffic backed up in queues on the motorway, and I see someone going nowhere in his rag-top Ferrari, shades on, and a super-model in the passenger seat, and steam coming out of his ears and his bonnet in equal measure, the mind does turn over the impact of a nice three pound rainbow at speed. No, you'd have to be there.

Little White Lies

Let's talk about big pheasants. I mean BIG pheasants. Not the fat pheasants which I have railed against on occasion, nor for that matter the big birds which are all those pheasants which are not the fast and furious Fenland variety that I know and love and chase with modest success. Nor even let us contemplate the big pheasants which we all recognise from time to time which turn out not to be pheasants at all, which explains why they looked big in the first place.

Guinea fowl fall into this category. More especially guinea fowl have a tendency to fall down where a perfectly acceptable pheasant went up. For those of you who still wake up in the deep heart of the night half consciously shredding the duvet as the tail-less hen falls victim to your powder and shot some sunny September afternoon, think only this of me – I thought it was a pheasant when it came divebombing out of the sun at me during the first drive after lunch. Guinea fowl are so peculiar, and surprisingly common on shoots (they are very good watchdogs and many a keeper has a few around his release pens). They certainly don't look like a pheasant, and yet at the same time, they don't actually not look like a pheasant. In the heat of the moment they don't anyway. Well, that's my story and I'm sticking to it.

For that matter think only kind thoughts of my friend – but no, I promised, really - anyway... who despatched a peahen in the midst of a tulgy wood as the dusk crept in upon him late in the season. Think not hard of him. It had been a long drive. It had been a longish day. And not the most exciting of outings. He was keen to engage. Well, we all are. You've been there. We all have. Brown blob comes wafting along through the trees, I mean, you apply a certain discretion. Not owls, certainly; never an owl. But owls flit. They don't bang into things. They veer this way and that in total silence with a spooky facility which almost automatically stays the hand. Not so your peahen, which comes blithering through the gloaming shrieking like a banshee and galumphing through the branches like a Chieftain tank gone bonkers in a bamboo plantation with all its crew wailing and gnashing teeth into the bargain. So the boy flattened it. Of course, the smoke had scarcely cleared before a melee of dogs descended upon the area in search of the corpse.

When you have just despatched with grace and elan the highest and fastest the estate has ever seen, it is strange how every retriever on the place is busy doing something important, like chatting up a cute little spaniel or laying a major multi-coiler on the ride; but when there is something that you would really not mind leaving exactly where it fell, Aw-hey-wey! Come by! Hi-lost! and pedigree chums in all directions. And it must be added, no sooner have you persuaded the victorious hound to part with its prize, which upon identification is speedily shoved down the nearest rabbit hole, warren or stump, than another of the brutes appears to re-retrieve what was not required to be retrieved in the first instance and deliver it with scarce concealed glee to its waiting owner who, with a relish which is unbecoming, in my view, in a professional, displays it to all and sundry thereby condemning the hapless Shot to seasons, perhaps a lifetime, of ribbing, japery and humiliation. Such as this piece, for instance. It's not even as if belting peahens, or guinea fowl for that matter, is against any particular law, such as I am aware of. It's just one of those things.

Anyway we're not going to talk about things like that are we? Although I did hear an interesting variation on the theme of white pheasant shooting. You all know the sort of thing. Host says "Please don't shoot the white pheasant; it's the keeper's wife's cousin's kid's pet." Or some such and then goes on to explain how any luckless Gun who does ambush the bird in question will be charged a forfeit which varies anywhere between dancing naked through the farmyard at lunch to real money.

Anyhow, the story goes that one host had cottoned to this idea as a bit of a money spinner on the side. White pheasants were off the card big time, with much tear-jerking explanation about keeper's infants raising the white chick from an egg and how the host had promised them on Granny's headstone that the bird would be forever preserved while breath there was in his bod. Being so habituated to humans, of course, the fateful bird tended to follow proceedings, so the Guns might encounter it on any drive, or indeed more than once. Special care was required. Hence his need, regretful but true, to fine any Gun who might despatch said fowl the price of £25, for the solace of the children of course.

The facts of the matter being, naturlicht, that the keeper and his unscrupulous host had flooded the place with white birds and were dividing the fines day by day as horror-stricken Guns paid up, sobbing, each thinking they had destroyed something unique. Come the day one of the Guns brings a guest, a man of some substance by all accounts if the gear and guns are any indicator. The host duly lays on his spiel about the white pheasant and the assembled company nod and mutter, as assembled companies are wont to do. The first couple of drives pass without incident, though it is manifestly the case that the bloke knows what he is about. Left and right, right and left. Fore and aft in that irritatingly effortless way which makes the rest of us so jealous. Doesn't seem to raise his gun unless there is the chance of popping a pair. A chance more often taken than not, I might add.

Last drive before lunch , the guest is delegated back gun and sent into the deep of the wood for the purpose. There follows a splendid drive for all the Guns with pheasants flying hither and yon as they are supposed to. High, wide and handsome. Much banging ensues, not least in the wood where the guest is clearly having a whale of a time and, if the rest of the morning is anything to go by, adding significantly to the bag as a consequence. The whistle goes, the smoke clears and from the back of the wood the guest appeared, his brows knitted in a frown reflecting inner turmoil. In his hand he held crumpled notes.

With what looked like tears welling in his eyes he approached the host. "Those poor children" says he " take this £25 to them forthwith with my apologies. It was a mistake, I assure you, I thought it an ordinary bird and shot at it early in the drive; but I must have only clipped it for the poor creature came over again shortly after. I was sure I put it out of any pain that time. Quite sure. Tell the children it did not suffer. Imagine my horror then when it appeared again." The Gun was almost weeping now. "I must have shot at that damn bird twenty times, and every time I was sure that I had killed it. It seemed to haunt me, coming back time after time. Anyway you will find its restless corpse behind my peg, assuming it came down at last. I did not have the heart to retrieve it myself. Please tell the children how sorry I am."

And with a broad wink at the other Guns, he pressed the £25 into the host's mitt and turned towards his vehicle. To rub salt in the wound when the keeper came through the wood, he found 20 white pheasants in a neat row beside the guest's peg. Petards, hoisting and own are words which spring to mind but you need some nerve to pull off a stunt like that. Plus you have to deliver the shooting end of matters into the bargain.

Anyway, let's talk about big pheasants. Well, sometime we will talk about big pheasants.

Creepy Behaviour

I was staying at a grandish sort of house the other weekend. Actually that's not fair. It's a biggish sort of a house, but not grand. Well, not in the frightfully, frightfully sense of the word; but it is big. And big presents a whole raft of problems which are better for being aired and shared.

Take this scenario for instance. Sunday morning I amble into my bathroom for the wakening tub. Large cast iron job in the middle of the room; ball and claw feet; splendid view from the window of the park falling away to the river; sunshine flooding hither and yon. You know how it is. Taps on, unguents in, bubbles in all directions. Tra-la! Test for temperature – and Whoa!! Horrors!! Stone cold.

Now here is the dilemma. I know that while all the baths are fired by a central boiler that is stoked day and night by some bloke who spends his life dragging logs into the bowels of the house to feed the brute. Therefore if my bath is a steam free zone, then even at this time of the morning, I know that there isn't a hot tub to be had in the house. However I also know that there is a shower room at the top of the house which, while not as luxurious as the bath mit unguents and view that I had been planning, will certainly achieve a satisfactory wake up pummel. The problem however strikes me even as I am halfway up the stairs with towel and sponge-bag.

You see, I know that the top floor rooms are occupied by the startlingly attractive girl who joined us for dinner last evening. I also know that our hosts occupy the bedroom at the foot of the stairs up which I am even now climbing.

The potential for social disaster floods in upon me like a Spey spate. One – slip into bathroom and surprise st. att. g in shower. Two - she squeaks prettily. Three - self seeks to explain perfectly understandable mistake while backing out of door. Four – towel catches in door and begins to unpeel revealing more of self than is proper, leading to more and enhanced squeaking from the shower cabinet. Five – hosts surprised from gentle slumbers by squeaking of st. att. g assemble at foot of stairs to

…revealing more of self than is proper.

be confronted by flustered, blushing, nude self. Six – explanations. Seven – reputation in tatters. Outlook – grim.

Now there may be those of you out there who view this as a somewhat pessimistic approach. "Why" you optimists propose "does he not look on the bright side? Why, for example, does the piece not end in whispered suggestiveness and, frankly, lewd expressions of mutual lath-erings? Now that would steam up a mirror or two; and brighten all our days into the bargain." Well, you may be sure that the thought crossed my mind as I sat on the stairs wondering how best to proceed. And the answer is that experience suggests that pessimism is a pretty sound approach. It may very well be that the ending is happier than one has contemplated, but it doesn't do to bank on it. So I am a pessimist. I'm English, after all. And I fish.

On the other hand, if the worst was going to happen, which it almost certainly was, then I should head back to my room pronto. However the chances now are that even as I head back down the stairs I shall meet the hosts on the landing. And what should my explanation be for creeping down the stairs from the top floor at this time of the morning in nothing but a bathtowel? You can see how that would be. If I carried on upwards however the best that could be expected would be to bump into the girl on the landing even as she headed for the bathroom and we all end up two paragraphs back. By now, of course, I wasn't even sure that I could remember which door upstairs actually led to the bath-room. This leads inevitably to my bursting into the SAG's bedroom clad in nothing but a bathtowel with all the dire consequences that entails.

Anyway there seemed, even at this juncture, to be little point in imitating the little mouse with clogs on, so I decided that nothing that was going to happen would be any the worse for my being clean and awake when it occurred, so I may as well make a bid for the shower and take my punishment like a man. A whimpering, begging and pleading sort of a man; but a man nonetheless. So I resumed my ascent of the stairs.

And do you know what happened? 'Course you don't. I'll tell you – nothing happened. I had a shower – very nice as a matter of fact – and never met a soul either on the way up or on the way down. No worries. So what is the point of all this? I'm not absolutely sure I know really.

I set out to advise the young and foolish, and lucky, among you on the proper etiquette of corridor creeping in big houses, but there doesn't seem to be room now. That being the case all I can advise, and we will go into this in more detail later, is that when creeping down corridors or scampering up and down stairs and confronted by hosts, staff or as it might be other guests in varying states of outrage, undress or even acute embarrassment the thing to do is state loudly and confidently "I am just going fishing." Which seems to excuse any madness. And keep moving.

Awaydays

It was all Nick's idea in the first place. Nick is a bit of a high pheasant specialist, and is always for going to the ends of the earth, if needs be, in pursuit of these archangels. I have fended off these suggestions in the past, not because I am afraid of being revealed as a low bird specialist in my own right, I am as keen as anyone to take on the sporting shot and devil take the hindmost. No, my objection lies in the fact that the ends of the earth tend to be a long and arduous trek, and long and arduous treks are not really my line.

However eventually I gave in, and accordingly decanted myself from a taxi at Kings Cross to undertake the exercise. I have addressed before the quantity of gear that is vital to a days shooting, and the sundry bags, suitcases, guncases, cartridge bags and dog beds that joined me on the rain slick pavement bore mute and weighty testimony to my complete inability to cut down the bare essentials to anything less than a small truckload. However Coco and I hijacked a trolley and were soon making our top-heavy progress towards departure.

I will not set down the details of the journey, since the slightest brush with British Rail tends to send my blood pressure sailing into the heart attack zone, and even the memory still causes me to go red in the face. If every passenger on the railways can think of fifty ways in which the service can be improved within seconds of finding their reserved seat occupied by someone else, why can't the management of the blasted trains not come up with one or two every decade? Anyhow we will gloss over the horrors of modern, well modernish, transport by saying that even Coco, who is a relatively picky traveller at the best of times, preferred to curl up on the floor for the duration, rather than occupy the expensive seat, when it was eventually vacated, that I had purchased for her.

Upon our arrival though things began to pick up. We were met on the platform, just as Nick had promised and within a few moments we were being wafted off into the Northumbrian countryside, and shortly afterwards found us turning through a pair of very superior gateposts indeed. A small tip for the uninitiated; do not assume that passing through the gate of what Nick describes as "an old house in the middle of nowhere" signals the end of your journey. If you begin to fidget and collect your belongings, and wake up the dog, and so forth, you will reveal your gruesome lack of familiarity with socking great country piles. The drives up to some of these places go on and on and on, and it may be many minutes of satisfactory gravel crunching before you finally arrive at the portcullis that is your final destination.

Once having come to a complete halt however, you may ease yourself from the motor and take stock of the surroundings. This was not easy in our case since it was pitch black and the surroundings seemed to stretch for ever in all directions. Coco eventually found what apppeared to be a front door, though it looked like a wall to me, and closer examination revealed a bell pull, about the size of a dinner plate, which seemed ludicrously small in relation to the door itself. While distant chimes announced our arrival I made my way back to the heap of belongings somewhere in the dark at the centre of the threshold. Footsteps, lights, action and hellos.

The door creaked open and there we were. Guests, host, dogs, introductions and a large tumbler of the necessary followed in quick succession and in no time flat Coco and I were ensconced before a suitably baronial roaring log fire and feeling increasingly comfortable. Dinner in the many galleried dining room and some rumbustiousness in the billiards room later and it was lights out in no uncertain terms in order to face the pheasants bright and early on the morrow.

It was, I am afraid to say, a rather subdued and distinctly unbright group of Guns who assembled in the great hall in the cold light of day. Several had failed the all important fried egg test at breakfast, and a few had even been fallers at the porridge hurdle; not an auspicious start. Nonetheless the team was looking better once we had assembled at the first drive. The sharp tang of the Northumbrian air was clearing several brains and lungs polluted by years of exposure to the diesel fumes of the No.9 bus were getting a dose of oxygen for a change. Not a big dose, mark you for as we drew numbers our host was explaining that we should take up position about halfway up a steep slope that looked to me as is it might easily finish what the rigours of the previous evening had started unless we were careful. Nick was lurking in the background wearing what can only be described as a knowing smile plastered across his face which should have given me some kind of clue. After toiling up the slope I settled the dog and set about getting myself organised. It was not going to be easy swinging on this sharp slope so I found myself a wee plateau and filled my pocket with cartridges and waited. I watched the brow of the hill where I expected the birds to appear and prepared to ambush the first pheasant foolish enough to stick its head over the parapet.

And that, of course, was my mistake. The pheasants did not stick their heads over the parapet, or the brow, or any other part of the hill at all. They weren't down here; they were up there. They took off from the far side of the hill, used the contours as a sort of launching ramp and had peaked out long before they cleared our side of the slope. They weren't going up any more, they were angling down and literally divebombing their way into the woods a quarter of a mile or so beyond and below us. They were gliding in a gravity-assisted swoop that began somewhere in the stratosphere and cleared the Guns at maximum range and increasing velocity. As they spotted the tiny figures dancing in the line below they stuck out the occasional wing, just for devilment, and swung abruptly left or right accordingly, and sometimes back again.

I missed the first one. I think it was the first one. It was certainly the first one I tried to shoot; there may have been others I ought to have tried for, but to be honest I was hoping something might arrive that I had some chance of connecting with. I felt something give in the clothing department on about the third attempt; could have been braces, maybe a sleeve. Hard to tell. There was a lot of banging going on up and down the line but not a lot to show for the fusillade.

I swung onto the next one harder and faster than I had ever swung in my shooting career to date. Either I would nail one of these birds or end the drive with a brace of hernias in the attempt. Possibly both. I put so much daylight between gun and bird that I had almost

I felt something give in the clothing department.

lost sight of the pheasant entirely. And I still missed it. Further, faster, harder still. Whatever had burst about the garments gave further, with a terrible rending sound as I loosed off the second barrel. The angle was impossible and the lead incredible. The result was unbelievable. The bird threw back its head and plunged through a long arc to arrive at the fence beside the wood behind us. It seemed to take forever. I watched it. Coco watched it. I hoped fervently that everyone else was watching it too.

I would like to relate that after this initial breakthrough I made short work of a stream of the highest birds. Alas, I cannot. There was a stream all right, of birds to be sure, but also of strong language as one after another they sailed by untouched. I did have more spectacular successes, but they were heavily outnumbered by spectacular double unsuccesses. Nick spent most of the day hauling down great quantities of these star-chasers, in between bouts of hysterical giggles. Ha!

I have however persuaded him to join me shortly out in the Fens. My territory, my birds. Not as high perhaps, but small and fast, with the feet permanently stuck in claggy plough. Deadly to the high bird specialist, or so I fondly hope. Then we will see who laughs last.

Tackle Monster

I met an old and wizened fisherman in the snug bar. He had wild hair and a ferocious beard and eyes which rolled horribly in opposite directions. And he had one of those waistcoats with little bits of sheepskin fluff here and there and more pockets and zips than you can shake a rod at. He had lures fixed in both ears. In fact he looked a bit like the great red bearded gillie on a Sunday morning after a bit of a bad night down at *The Leisterer's Retreat*. He beckoned me closer with a horny finger so obviously I pretended I hadn't seen him because buying pints in order to hear old fishermen's lies is a trick I've learned to dodge over the years. But he beckoned me again and like a salmon with the lure right in the angle I was inevitably drawn nearer and nearer. As we closed he grabbed my wrist in his leathery claw and bawled beerily into my face. "Beware the tackle monster, my boy, as you value your soul and your sanity!"

I leapt as if gaffed and shot the better part of a working half down my front. Then he fell back against the settle and stared vaguely into his glass. From time to time he muttered "Beware!" again and dribbled a good deal.

I tell you this because the Game Fair is coming up. More particularly the game fair season is almost upon us and Fisherman's Row, indeed Rows, beckon siren-like to the passing angler.

Now you know and I know that in order to partake of the sacred brotherhood of the angle all that is required is a whippy sort of stick, some string and a bent pin. Everything else is just gadgets and showing off. Well, perhaps a landing net, too. And a priest is only fair. And a pair of long nose forceps. And a box of spare pins. And something to bend them with. In a little leather pouch, of course. And some more string. Which might as well go on a reel, I suppose. With a bag to keep all of this in, obviously. Waders are a help and the coat and hat are not just for fishing after all and a life jacket is only sensible and cases for the rods are a boon and those things to keep rods on cars and more rods and more reels and more cases and a floating line and a sinking line and a forward taper sink tip and a matching set of fly boxes and a doodah and a thingummy and a widget and one of those cutting edge, NASA designed, Kevlar graphite bonded, not available in any shops, one-time, direct to you, small deposit secures, no holds barred, elbow your way to the front of the queue, impress your friends, refillable, self inflating, one off, Game Fair special price, easy payment terms, saw it in a magazine whatsit which none of us can remember the name of but which none of us can live without. Period. And I want it today.

Beware the tackle monster! It lurks within us all and all it takes to bring it roaring forth is a glass or two of lunch, a wallet and a walk down Fisherman's Row.

I am, of course, as guilty as any of us. In fact, probably more so in that I make a point of buying things which do not promise to catch me more fish or bigger. Somewhere deep in my protestant, almost Presbyterian, soul there is a voice which tells me that using gadgets to catch more fish and bigger is both unfair on the fish and unsporting to my fellow anglers. I insist therefore on using old rods with rusty reels, snaggly lines and moth-eaten lures. At least until the *Trout and Salmon* Editor issues me with something better I do anyhow.

On the other hand that is no reason not to have pockets full of hook sharpeners, line straighteners, knot unpickers, line greasers and de-greasers, disgorgers, pincers, tweezers, forceps, non toxic weight dispensers, clippers, gauges, thermometers, lighters, sunglasses, potions, elixirs, guaranteed thises and that's endorsed by anglers and sports psychiatrists both here and in the United States. Well, is it?

I am in addition somewhat sensitive on this issue because my father, the Aging Progenitor, in one of his occasional fits of mortality confrontation, decided to unload yet another tsunami of his redundant fishing gear in my direction. I had to chuckle, as I went through it, at some of the rubbish he'd been fobbed off with over a long and illustrious career as a Mark I tackle monster.

It was only later that the truth struck me with a resounding thump like an Ally Shrimp between the shoulderblades. I had laughed when I saw this useless stuff but did I hurl the whole festering pile

A ferocious beard and eyes that rolled in opposite directions.

straight at the dustmen? I did not. Did I heave the bulk of his belongings toward the nearest junk shop? Nope. Did I burn it and consign the ashes to a watery rest in the pond? Not a hope. I added his lot to my own. I had a lot of stuff. He gave me more. I have accumulated a great deal. He has now given me the rest. I now have at least twice what he had had at his peak. And the game fair season is almost upon us. Run! Save yourselves!

Tackle monsterr**rrrrr** !!

The Season Past

I like to think that with each passing year I grow a little wiser as well as a little older. That with the close of each shooting season I have inched forward a tiny distance and have gained some shred of wisdom worth passing on.

This year I really think I have cracked it. Not shooting as a whole perhaps; there aren't enough lessons in a day or days in a year to achieve that, but I do think I have put a vital piece in the puzzle over the last three months or so.

You know those Guns who come back from every drive with a brace or two? Even when they are out on the flank? Even when you put them there yourself in the certain knowledge that they would not get to shoot a thing? And yet they still get a few shots and still come marching up, grinning like idiots, and carrying a couple or three pheasants. And when you ask if they had a few shots then, they answer non-committally, "Oh several actually." Only you heard them banging away like a small war zone when by rights they should have been doing nothing whatever. I hate those guys. Really I do.

And yet I have now become one of them. Because I know how it is done. Two ways I learned this. Let me tell you.

First I was invited partridge shooting. Late September, or it might have been early October. Whatever. I drew a peg between two Guns who were noted Shots to start with and who had just returned from three weeks of driven grouse shooting into the bargain. Three weeks! Some people, eh? Before the first drive, one of the pickers up mentioned out of the side of his mouth, just in passing, that I would have to look sharp about it if I wanted any shooting today, because these boys were something to see, and having had three weeks at the grouse, were not about to slow down for my benefit.

Well, I am as much a man as the next for picking up gauntlets when I see them and so you can be sure that I was not in a mood to take prisoners as we took our pegs. Bo-Boom! on my left and Ba-Bang! on

245

my right. Two brace bouncing on the stubbles as the first covey hurtled through, and I didn't even get a shot off. I took one out of the next covey, but missed with my second barrel, only to see two more birds crumple behind me, thoroughly dead, at distances well beyond where I would have thought to shoot. And so the day progressed. They weren't rude, they didn't poach. They simply shot harder and better than I did. All day.

Now with this in mind I went to the shooting school, and when my instructor asked what my pleasure was to be, I did not opt for the floating, middle of the ride, middle of the road, overhead driven bird. "Let us," I announced "focus on the marginal bird. The bird the average Gun does not shoot." And so we did.

We paced out forty yards, from the high tower, and shot crossing targets, at forty yards plus. Or rather he did. I kept missing. "They are out of range!" says I. "You just can't hit them!" says he. And to prove the point he takes my gun and shoots four out of the next five. I suspect he left the last one so as not to depress me completely. Then I tried some more. And it is a strange thing but once you hit one, you can do it forever. Once you have absorbed the fact that at this range there is more to life than swinging through and letting off, that is. Out here you have to swing on, and on, and on, and a bit more besides. But it can be done. And once you know how, you too can be one of those irritating people who always get a brace. You do get through a great number of cartridges. I daresay I shot twice as many squibs this season as last; but I collected a good deal more game for them too.

Now don't misunderstand me on this. I am not advocating letting off at things in the next county. Let's not get stupid about the whole thing. But forty yards is further than you think and certainly a lot further than many Guns will shoot.

For instance. Last shoot of the season. The Guns are set out thirty five yards back from the wood's edge. A pheasant gets up well back and swings along the line across the tree tops by Number Two. He cries "Over!" and does nothing. Three, Four and Five all shout "Over!" to one another and also do nothing. I am number Seven. I shout to Number Six, on my left, to shoot, but he watches the bird whizz by without raising his gun. So I shot it. Improved cylinder. 28g standard 16 bore cartridge. Dead as you like. They all said "What a wonderful shot!" It wasn't. Not at all. It was a straightforward shot that they were all disinclined to attempt. They all use 12 bores so any one of them might have expected to do the same. I did it twice more during the drive and was still the only Gun to let off. At the end of the drive I had a couple of brace in all, which was as many as anyone.

This is what I have learned: I can't shoot any better than the others, but I can let off more. And the more I send up, the more I bring down. It's no secret.

"You just can't hit them", says he.

Pigeon Pursuits

I am not a big pigeon shooter.

Oh, I am happy enough to go and take my place in some copse, spinney or plantation during the big shoots of February or March, and to let off a pop now and again to keep the flocks on the move while those more organised than myself busy themselves with yards of camouflage netting, and oil drums, and sitty trees, and flappers and floaters, and poles and the like; but I am not, when all is said, done, set out, timed and decoyed, a pigeon shooter in the truest sense of the word.

"Time spent in reconaissance is seldom wasted!" If I've heard that once I've heard it a hundred times. There is little doubt that it is is true, but it is a motto of little value if the call comes before you have managed to do any of your actual reconnaisance. "Get yourself into the pines at the end of Big Wood around three-ish and keep on until dark."

248

coming in the middle of lunch does not give you a bundle of time for reconnaissance. As a matter of fact it does not give you anything more than time to swallow what you have in front of you, grab gun and bullets and make your way to the allotted spot with boundless ambition and terminal indigestion.

The fact that you have stood here, in this very spot, on the last drive of a late pheasant day only a couple of weeks previously watching pigeons piling into this actual tree as if their lives depended on it, does not count as reconnaisance, because that was then and this is now. And now they are piling in some several hundred yards away and there is nothing you can do about it except up-sticks and wander forlornly along the edge of said pines in a desperate attempt to get under what appears to be an established flight line. With the book of rules in one hand and a machete in the other you attempt to create for yourself an effective hide from the resources available to you and sconce yourself in a position where one might be able to do a bit of good, but after finally letting off a few shots, more in hope than anger, at birds that are floating about in the stratosphere, the thought inevitably occurs that you are in the wrong place at the wrong time, and the only answer is to move to somewhere else. Again. And again.

I have read, marked, learned and inwardly digested all the available advice on how to get on equal terms with the pigeon as wily adversary and I have to say that all those wise and successful pigeon shooters who have offered of their wisdom, must surely have been up against a different bird altogether than the distant grey floaters that I am consistently confronted with.

I check out lines of approach. They change it. I put up a number of decoys. This in itself is an exercise of considerable difficulty that is largely skated over in the advice handed out to the aspiring pigeon shooter. I do not, I freely admit, carry about a set of scaffolding that would easily permit the lofting of an attractive pattern of several well stuffed decoys. But then again, who does? How, exactly, do these experts hoist their deeks into the canopy of a wood that may easily be dozens of feet aloft? Is a set of chimney sweeping brushes obligatory? I have tried lobbing balls of string into the upper branches of dead trees and, for that matter, not so dead trees. But whereas in the book the effect is a neatly assembled pattern of attractive lures, when I try it all that is achieved is what appears to be a tree full of badly sorted laundry, an eye full of twig, and a torn shoulder from persistant lobbing of balls of increasingly tangled twine. The net result looks like a badly decorated Christmas tree guarded by a disabled elf. Maybe a tennis raquet would help. I would certainly be no worse off. I can't play tennis, of course, but then I am no great pigeon shot either.

All this talk of flight lines. What exactly does a flight line consist of? In my wood all the pigeons seem to take a pretty cavalier attitude towards flight lines. If one comes in from one direction, then the next veers in from a completely different angle. Number three swans in from some distant field of num-num delicious crops while the fourth simply meanders about looping the loop and practising windage-sideslip from a safe distance. Two in a row over the same tree makes a line; until I am under it, at which point it becomes a coincidence never to be repeated. Until, that is, I have moved elsewhere.

Now there may be those among you who are skilled and acknowl-edged pigeon shooters. A boon to your local farmers and game dealers alike; who seldom stir from your chair for less than a bag of fifty or more, and who keep a van permanently stocked with guns, cartridges, netting, decoys, maps and poles on the off chance that the call should come. To you, I wish nothing but the best of sport and luck.

To those, however, who have have spent many a long evening in some colossal wood, pooping off at forty minute intervals at some distant bird in the hope that something might eventually happen within striking distance, I say "You are not alone, crouched under your bush." For my own part I very shortly undertake what might be called the Close Combat Approach.

This involves rounding up the two nearest Guns, who are equally crouched despondently under their bush in other parts of the wood, and forming a roving patrol to wander up and down the rides. It is important that all Guns in the vicinity are involved because the last thing you want is bushes containing fellow Guns lurching into view at the last minute, enquiring as to what is going on. Having accumulated the team (three is ideal), two face forward and one stumbles along in reverse gear, and all three stomp up and down the rides with little or no concern for noise abatement. The result is that pigeons who had happily installed themselves in the wood for the night are abruptly dislodged from their roosts and zoom out of the trees in all directions. The right hand Gun takes left hand birds, and the Gun on the left takes right hand birds. That, at least is the theory. The backfacing Gun takes late starters, which calls for really quick reactions and spot on accuracy. For an hour or so before dusk this combination can have a lot of fun in blatant contradiction of everything the books say about pigeon shooting, and none the worse for that.

It may be closer to the OK Corral style than one would ordinarily wish for, but it can be a bundle of fun; and if we were properly organised, equipped and camoflaged pigeon shooters we would not be wandering around this great big wood six weeks after everyone else, without a pole or a decoy between us, with a bag full of empty cartridges and not a feather to show for it. So there. Now who's for a stroll about.

How to Survive Gamefairs

Isolate the problems, and as often as not the answer will appear in shimmering certainty right under your nose. And what is the biggest problem posed by gamefairs in general, or indeed a game fair in particular? Getting there comes top of my list. The prospect of sitting for endless hours in queues of traffic waiting to arrive at the chosen venue appals me. I may have no very clear idea of why I want to go, or what I am going to do when I get there; but I do know that whatever it is, it doesn't start until after arrival and that time spent en route is time wasted.

The simple solution is to accumulate, whether by purchase or inheritance, a huge and impractical country pile and letting out the grounds to passing gamefairs in exchange for free passage. The people who motor slowly round and round gamefairs in a beaten up farm truck with a badge stuck under the windscreen wiper saying "Owner." seem to me to have the thing pretty much taped. Failing this, the more modest route is to propose oneself for the weekend with the folk who do own the pile in question, or as a final choice to lodge with friends who live no distance flat from the scene of activities. This allows travelling time to be cut to a minimum and also means that you can be among the earliest of arrivals at the fair without having to set off from home several days in advance.

Early arrival is critical. Not only does it mean that the crowds which develop during the day can be largely avoided by being left consistently one step behind, but it also means that one can park as close as may be permitted to the centre of operations. Some fairs now have a sort of priority booking system where by paying extra money special arrangements can be secured. This is well worth the additional pounds as anyone who has lost their transport in what has become hundreds of acres of liquids mud will soon tell you. Pay whatever they ask. If it means having to walk less and carry things not at all, it will be cheap at the price.

The other reason for arriving first thing is winning things. Or if not actually winning things then at least leading the field. This was

…before the judges had even got their stop watches synchronised.

a wheeze that Coco and I stumbled upon in our competitive period. Coco was a star of the scurries, and even some more advanced retrieving competitions; but as the days wore on and more dogs went round the course, Coco found that they left behind things more interesting by far than dummies. Accordingly much time would be spent addressing herself to the pursuit of new friends and wandering off among the spectators than responding to the increasingly frantic whistlings and wavings of yours truly. By going first however, before the judges had even got their stop watches synchronised and sunk the first coffee of what could be a long, hot and difficult day, not only were these distractions avoided, but we also got our names on the leader board. Or at least until the second competitor had completed the course we did. The same can be applied to shooting competitions, fly-casting, pigeon plucking, decoy carving, tent erecting and any number of other challenges to the sportsperson. We do all of them, in quick order, pose briefly by the trophy with our names in lights, record the moment for posterity and then zoom off to the shops.

I don't buy anything really. It is sometimes possible to snag a bargain before the traders are fully awake, but whereas it used to be the case that special offers at the gamefair meant a lower price than usual, it seems now that the reverse is often true. Nonetheless there are usually some super new gadgets on display and the key here is to examine things closely, point out their glaring defects to a startled proprietor and trouser a brochure or card and order the product later from the comfort and calm of home. It is a good test of a new product that if the advertising material lingers long enough for me to get round to buying something, then it is probably something worth buying.

By now it should be getting on for lunchtime and this is a central part of gamefairing. There was a time when nothing more was required at this point than a quick swoop round the tents of the high street banks, where a flash of the chequebook was a signal for fawning managers to descend from all sides with chilled glasses and an abundance of salads. It is a sad reflection on our times that these days one is lucky to get a warm can of fizzy drink and a record token. Perhaps it is just my own deteriorating relationship with banks, but I am led to believe it is general. Nil desperandum though, the Gazette tent should have a little something, and the BFSS is usually good for an aperatif or twain. Then to the picnic.

Technology has made picnics a joy. No more sweaty sandwiches and melted biccies; warm beer and cold coffee. UGH! Nightmares past. Now from the boot of the motor comes a stream of insulated boxes, and the baskets give forth proper linens and cutlery. Tankards are the best thing for drinks, whether wines, beers or cordials; even, should the weather be inclement, a warming soup. They do not fall over, they are indestructible and they hold a decent quantity. Hot things in one box; cold things in another. Cold cucumber soup, boned fowl, smoked pheasant, venison terrine, cheese, pickles and salads from the chilled side; spiced chowder, chicken wings, sausages, hot rolls and relishes from the hot box. A selection of seasonal fruits with plenty of whipped cream and meringues for afters should see the job done. Icy white wines for the heat and a chewy claret if it is overcast would be my choice. Beer is a reasonable bet, but can lead to tense moments in the latter parts of the day, and the number of conveniences at gamefairs as compared with the number of inconveniences is legendary. Boys have specialised equipment in this department but due regard should be given to all members, if that is not an inopportune description, of the party.

Finally, don't forget the dog. Or better still do. Unless you are intending to compete actively as a duo, or give a demonstration on the do's or more probably don'ts of canine obedience and training, leave the unhappy creature at home. For a dog gamefairs are either hot, crowded, dull and frustrating or cold, crowded, dull and frustrating. If you don't believe me, next time you go to a party spend thirty minutes on your hands and knees and count how many times you are kicked, trodden on and occasionally molested by strangers. Then go and lock yourself in the car for four or five hours and see how it feels. If you are competing, or demonstrating or whatever, then bring refreshments for the hound, and a bowl to put them in. Yours may indeed be the best dog in the world, in the universe, in space but I have yet to come across the dog that can manage a can opener or a straw unaided.

Departure should be a re-run of arrival. Organisers are getting much better at traffic management as a matter of fact but jams still occur. Look for the neglected back route and do not be shy about going in the opposite direction from the masses. Slow and steady may win races, but sneaky and peculiar often gets home first from the gamefair.

On the other hand of course, if you do happen to own the park, it is merely a question of pulling the door closed behind you and reaching for the decanter on the sideboard. Think about the lawn mowing though...